THE SECURE BASE MODEL

Promoting attachment and resilience in foster care and adoption

Gillian Schofield and Mary Beek

Published by
CoramBAAF Adoption and Fostering Academy
41 Brunswick Square
London WC1N 1AZ
www.corambaaf.org.uk

Charity registration 275689 (England and Wales) and SC039337 (Scotland)

© Gillian Schofield and Mary Beek, 2014

Reprinted 2020

British Library Cataloguing in Publication Data
A catalogue record for this book is available from the British Library

ISBN 978 1 907585 83 8

Project management by Shaila Shah, Publisher, BAAF
Photograph on cover from istockphoto.com
Designed and typeset by Helen Joubert Design
Printed in Great Britain by The Lavenham Press
Trade distribution by Turnaround Publisher Services, Unit 3,
Olympia Trading Estate, Coburg Road, London N22 6TZ

BAAF is the leading UK-wide membership organisation for all those
concerned with adoption, fostering and child care issues.

Contents

Notes about the authors   v

Acknowledgements   vi

1 Introduction   **1**

Secure Base – a framework for caregiving   1

International developments   3

Using Secure Base in practice   3

2 Attachment and resilience concepts   **4**

Attachment formation   4

A secure base   6

Internal working models   6

Mind-mindedness   7

Attachment and resilience   8

The impact of abuse and neglect   9

Secure and insecure attachment patterns   9

The importance of a secure base   11

3 Secure Base   **13**

The caregiving cycle   13

Dimensions of caregiving   14

Availability – helping the child to trust   17

Sensitivity – helping the child to manage feelings   20

Acceptance – building the child's self-esteem   24

Co-operation – helping the child to feel effective   28

Family membership – helping the child to belong   31

4 Using Secure Base: assessing prospective foster carers and adopters   **36**

Availability – helping the child to trust   37

Sensitivity – helping the child to manage feelings 38

Acceptance – building the child's self-esteem 39

Co-operation – helping the child to feel effective 40

Family membership – helping the child to belong 41

5 Using Secure Base: assessing the capacity of caregivers to provide a secure base for children in their care **43**

The Secure Base Interview 44

Analysis of the Secure Base Interview 48

6 Using Secure Base: supporting caregivers **57**

Introducing the caregiving cycle 58

Exploring each Secure Base dimension with caregivers 58

Availability – helping the child to trust 58

Sensitivity – helping the child to manage feelings 60

Acceptance – building the child's self-esteem 61

Co-operation – helping the child to feel effective 63

Family membership – helping the child to belong 64

7 Using Secure Base: assessing and reviewing the development of fostered and adopted children **66**

Framework for assessment 67

Secure Base Checklist 67

Frequently Asked Questions **77**

References **80**

Resources **82**

Secure Base Summary Chart 82

Secure Base Progress Record 83

Secure Base star 84

Secure Base – caregiving cycle and dimensions 85

Secure Base – Guide to the DVD **91**

Notes about the authors

Gillian Schofield is Professor of Child and Family Social Work and Head of the School of Social Work at the University of East Anglia (UEA). An experienced social worker, she has a special interest in attachment theory and child placement and has researched and published widely in this field.

Mary Beek has had a long and varied career in fostering and adoption practice for Norfolk County Council, and research and publication in the Centre for Research on Children and Families. She has recently completed work on a longitudinal follow-up study of adopted children at UEA, led by Elsbeth Neil, and is currently the Training and Quality Assurance Manager for Care for Children.

Gillian Schofield and Mary Beek have worked closely together on a series of projects at the Centre for Research on Children and Families since 1997, undertaking research and developing the Secure Base model for understanding and supporting the role of foster carers and adopters in caring effectively for children.

Books by the same authors

Schofield G and Beek M (2014) *Promoting Attachment and Resilience: A guide for foster carers and adopters on using the Secure Base Model*, London: BAAF

Schofield G, Biggart L, Ward E, Scaife V, Dodsworth J, Haynes A, and Larsson P (2014) *Looked after Children and Offending: Reducing risk and promoting resilience*

Schofield G and Simmonds J (eds) (2009) *The Child Placement Handbook: Theory, research and practice*, London: BAAF

Schofield G and Beek M (2008) *Achieving Permanence in Foster Care*, London: BAAF

Schofield G, Ward E, Warman A, Simmonds J and Butler J (2008) *Permanence in Foster Care: A study of care planning and practice in England and Wales*, London: BAAF

Schofield G and Beek M (2006) *Attachment for Foster Care and Adoption*, London: BAAF

Schofield G and Beek M (2006) *Attachment Handbook for Foster Care and Adoption: A training programme*, London: BAAF

Beek M and Schofield G (2004) *Providing a Secure Base in Long-term Foster Care*, London: BAAF

Schofield G (2003) *Part of the Family: Pathways through foster care*, London: BAAF

Schofield G, Beek M and Sargent K with Thoburn J (2000) *Growing up in Foster Care*, London: BAAF

Howe D, Brandon M, Hinings D and Schofield G (1999) *Attachment Theory, Child Maltreatment and Family Support: A practice and assessment model*, Basingstoke: Macmillan

Acknowledgements

We are grateful to the Nuffield Foundation for funding a series of research projects from 1997–2010 that have helped us to develop the Secure Base model. We would also like to thank the Esmée Fairbairn Foundation and the Gulbenkian Foundation for funding the development work that led to the *Attachment Handbook for Foster Care and Adoption* (2006) on which much of the subsequent work has built.

From the world of practice, we are very grateful to all the social workers from a range of agencies who have shown interest and enthusiasm for developing the Secure Base model. We particularly appreciate the contribution of Toril Havik from Bergen University and the group of Norwegian practitioners – Louise Brattlie, Joachim Brotkorb, Ole Jørgensen, Jori Skulstad and Egil Skundberg – who have brought their considerable commitment and expertise to implementing and developing the Secure Base Model across Norway since 2006.

Finally, we would like to thank all the foster carers and adoptive parents who have shown us how providing a secure base for troubled children can help them to fulfil their potential.

1 Introduction

All children of all ages need to feel secure in their relationships with the adults who look after them. A secure base is at the heart of any successful family environment. It is provided through a loving relationship with caregivers who offer the child sensitive care and protection, but also a reliable base from which to explore and enjoy their world. Thus a secure base relationship promotes not only a sense of security, but also confidence, competence and resilience.

Secure Base – a framework for caregiving

Since 2000, the authors, Gillian Schofield and Mary Beek of the Centre for Research on Children and Families at the University of East Anglia, have been developing and applying to fostering and adoption practice a framework for caregiving: the **Secure Base** model. The model is founded on key theories and research about child development and family relationships – and also on what we have learned from child placement research. All children need sensitive caregiving, but children who come into foster and adoptive families are likely to have experienced backgrounds of abuse and neglect, as well as separation and loss, and need a special kind of therapeutic caregiving.

The Secure Base model has its roots in theory and research on attachment, but also on resilience. The goal of the model is to provide sensitive caregiving that develops secure close relationships. These relationships help children to recover from previous harmful experiences in close relationships. This enables them to feel competent to face future challenges successfully and to fulfil their potential. Resilience is associated with a sense of security, self-esteem, self-efficacy, a capacity to reflect on feelings, and hopefulness for the future – all key characteristics of secure attachment. Resilience, like security, can be promoted in the context of a sensitive and responsive caregiving environment. It is this positive, strengths-based approach to family relationships that is at the heart of this model of caregiving.

Secure Base can be used in a number of different areas of professional practice with children and families. But it is particularly valuable in family placement, where children can experience sensitive and available care that provides the foundation of secure attachment relationships, builds resilience and enables children to thrive in their families, peer groups, education and communities.

The model brings together five dimensions of caregiving. These five dimensions interact with each other to create a secure base for the child. The first four dimensions of caregiving – *availability, sensitivity, acceptance* and *co-operation* – come from the work of one of the earliest attachment researchers, Mary Ainsworth (1971, 1978). She found in her study of infants that these four caregiving dimensions were associated with secure attachment. The fifth dimension, *family membership*, has been added to the model because of its significance for all children, but especially for children separated from their families of origin and developing new family memberships in their foster and adoptive families. The family membership dimension focuses on the child's need for a sense of belonging in their new family that still takes account of their connection with their birth family.

Research at the University of East Anglia (for example, Beek and Schofield, 2004, Schofield and Beek, 2009) extended the application of Ainsworth's dimensions from infancy through childhood to adolescence, suggesting that, although these dimensions may be expressed differently at different ages, they perform the same function for the child. For example, in both infancy and adolescence the availability of a caregiver is necessary to build trust.

As well as extending the age range, the research suggested that there were some specific developmental benefits to each dimension of caregiving, and that these could become a focus for assessing children's development and progress, which in turn would inform the support needed for the caregivers.

The publication by BAAF of the *Attachment Handbook for Foster Care and Adoption* (Schofield and Beek, 2006) set out the five caregiving dimensions in some detail. It also offered practitioners and caregivers an account of attachment patterns from infancy to adolescence, with an emphasis on what children with insecure attachments bring to their placements and what they might therefore need from caregivers. It highlighted both the challenges and the rewards that caregivers will find as they help children to feel more secure. The book provided ideas about applications of attachment principles and Secure Base to assessing and placing children; recruiting and preparing new foster carers and adopters; managing children's behaviour difficulties; and contact.

In 2007, the Government policy document, *Care Matters*, described Secure Base as helping to promote confidence and competence in children and it was recommended for training and supporting foster carers. In 2008, the model provided a foundation for a Good Practice Guide, *Achieving*

Permanence in Foster Care, and a website was developed to provide downloadable materials (www.uea.ac.uk/providingasecurebase). In 2009, Secure Base was incorporated in *Skills to Foster*, the training programme for new carers developed by the Fostering Network.

This practice guide has been developed to bring together both explanatory material about Secure Base and the range of resources that are available to help social workers put it into practice. A separate volume for foster carers and adopters is also available.

International developments

From 2006 Secure Base also started to be adopted by fostering teams in Norway, translated as *Trygg Base*. It was then included, as in the UK, as part of the Norwegian national training programme for new foster carers and has been used regularly in practice since.

The continuing international interest in the application of attachment theory to family placement practice led to the *Attachment Handbook for Foster Care and Adoption* being translated into French (2011) and Italian (2013).

Using Secure Base in practice

As this practice guide will show, there are many areas of social work practice in child placement that can benefit from this systematic way of thinking about, describing and assessing key qualities of caregiving and key dimensions of child development.

Examples provided in this guide are:

- assessing prospective foster carers and adopters;
- assessing the capacity of caregivers to provide a secure base for children in their care;
- supporting caregivers; and
- assessing and reviewing the child's development and progress.

These elements of practice can be brought together to inform other areas of practice; for example, the assessment of caregivers and children using Secure Base dimensions can inform matching. It can also inform the assessment of the support that a placement might need to succeed.

The focus here is on practical everyday parenting and on working collaboratively with foster carers and adoptive parents to maximise their capacity to care effectively for children from backgrounds of abuse and neglect.

2 Attachment and resilience concepts

Secure Base is founded on attachment theory. An in-depth knowledge of attachment theory and research is not essential for practitioners or caregivers to use the model, but an understanding of some of the basic concepts of attachment is helpful. Here we provide brief summaries of the attachment concepts that are particularly relevant to the model, including the link between attachment and resilience.

- Attachment formation
- Secure base
- Internal working models
- Mind-mindedness
- Attachment and resilience
- Impact of abuse and neglect
- Secure and insecure attachment patterns
- The importance of a secure base

Attachment formation

The starting point of John Bowlby's theory of attachment is an evolutionary one, in that babies are seen as having a biological drive to *seek proximity* to an adult, usually the primary caregiver or caregivers, in order to survive danger (1969, 1973, 1980). The goal for the infant of this drive for closeness is to feel safe, secure and protected. This leads to a range of proximity-promoting *attachment behaviours*.

Attachment behaviours may attract the caregiver's attention in a positive way, for example, cooing, smiling and reaching out. But attachment behaviours will include protest behaviours, such as crying and fretting, which will also bring the caregiver closer in order to soothe the child and end the behaviour. In the toddler years, attachment behaviours will include more direct actions, such as approaching, following, clinging and other behavioural strategies that can achieve proximity to the attachment figure.

All of these attachment behaviours give strong signals that should lead caregivers to respond to the needs of the baby or the older child. In the first months of life, the signals from the baby are repeated and need to be responded to countless times each day. When the baby is hungry, lonely or uncomfortable, the sensitive and responsive caregiver will both recognise and react promptly to meet the baby's needs. This experience of having needs recognised and met provides a secure base that settles the baby and reduces his anxiety, which, in turn, allows him to play and explore. When the baby is relaxed, smiling and playful, the caregiver will also share and reinforce this mood. Through the process of attachment behaviours being responded to promptly and appropriately, the baby's survival is ensured, and his emotional, social and physical development is enhanced and maximised in the context of the relationship. Recent research has shown that sensitive caregiving is also necessary to promote healthy brain development in the first two years of life (Howe, 2011).

As attachment behaviours become more organised and demands for food or play become more targeted, the adults who respond to them become highly significant to the growing baby. In optimal conditions, attachment behaviours become linked with strong feelings of joy and delight in both the child and the caregiver. Caregivers, of course, respond to the needs and demands of their children in different ways and this gives rise to the different secure and insecure attachment patterns discussed below.

Selective attachments, then, begin to form from birth. Early infancy is a particularly sensitive period for their development, but there are further opportunities throughout childhood. During the toddler years, where there has been continuity of sensitive care, mobility, play and language develop, providing opportunities to extend attachment relationships to other close adults. Children of this age, who have not experienced sensitive care and move to a new foster or adoptive family, can develop secure attachments to new caregivers if the caregivers provide sensitive care.

By the age of three or four, another shift occurs as secure children become able to think about their own and other people's thoughts and feelings – which is key to their ability to manage relationships not only with adults but also with peers.

During the pre-school and primary years, secure children develop the capacity to hold the selective secure base relationships in mind when they are separated from family caregivers (for example, at nursery or school), leaving them free to explore and learn, but also able to turn to other trusted adults for support if needed. Also during this stage, children who are experiencing sensitive parenting continue to learn to manage their feelings, co-operate with others and take into account the thoughts and feelings of others in more complex ways.

During adolescence, secure young people are becoming increasingly confident and competent. Their thinking is more complex and more reflective and they can anticipate the future. There may be experimentation with the rejection of parental norms and values and moving away from the secure base, but family ties, parental pleasure in their successes, and the knowledge that the secure base is still available in times of difficulty remain very important.

The formation and development of attachment relationships continue through the lifespan, so that adult children's relationships with their parents will change and in romantic attachment relationships we both care for and receive care from our partners – becoming both care seekers and caregivers. The transition to parenthood requires a mature transformation into a caregiver who can provide a secure base for a child, although parents still need support from their own secure base in partners, adult relatives or friends.

A secure base

A secure base is provided through a relationship with one or more sensitive and responsive attachment figures who meet the child's needs and to whom the child can turn as a safe haven, when upset or anxious (Bowlby, 1988). When children develop trust in the availability and reliability of this relationship, their anxiety is reduced and they can therefore explore and enjoy their world, safe in the knowledge that they can return to their secure base for help if needed.

The concept of a secure base is essential to our understanding of relationship formation and children's development. It links attachment and exploration, and provides the basis of a secure attachment. A securely attached child does not only seek comfort from an attachment figure, but by feeling safe to explore, develops confidence, competence and resilience.

Internal working models

To understand the lessons that children learn in early relationships and why they go on to affect subsequent relationships, Bowlby developed the concept of "internal working models". An internal working model is a set of expectations and beliefs about the self, about others and about relationships. Thus, the internal working model of an individual will contain particular expectations and beliefs:

- Am I loveable and worthy of love?

● Are other people available, interested and able to help/protect/support me?

Internal working models begin to form in early infancy. If, for example, the baby finds that his feelings of hunger and his accompanying crying behaviour result in a prompt response from a loving adult who makes him feel better, he will learn that certain of his behaviours are linked with the positive behaviours of his caregiver. At the same time, he will feel that he is loved and nurtured and that he "deserves" this response. A more generalised expectation of adults as people who are likely to be there to help and protect also develops over time. At the other end of the spectrum, a parental response that is unavailable or cold will lead to an internal working model of the attachment figure as rejecting, the self as unworthy of care, and others as not to be relied on for help and support.

The models are termed "working" models because they are subject to change and development according to changing experiences in relationships. Bowlby observed that these models are established in the first few years of life, and as children get older, models retain some flexibility but do become increasingly resistant to change. This means that foster care and adoption need to provide family environments that are able to stick with troubled children who take time to learn to trust. But if families can offer this, then children's working models can change in a positive direction right through adolescence.

Children's behaviours become organised around their expectations of themselves and others and, as they grow older, these expectations tend to influence the way in which others relate to them. In this way, positive and negative cycles of reinforcement are set up. For example, the child who feels good about himself and expects others to be mostly warm and friendly will present himself to a potential friendship group in a way that signals 'You can trust me. I will be a good friend', and so elicits a positive response. Conversely, a child who expects rejection, has low self-esteem and a sense of the world as a hostile place is likely to signal defiantly 'I don't need or want your friendship, don't come close to me', which tends to bring about further rejection of the kind the child most fears. Positive internal working models can cope with a degree of rejection. Negative internal working models tend to see hostility even in neutral behaviour. Thus to change children's negative expectations of self and others requires caregivers who can sustain availability and sensitive responding in the face of apparent hostility and lack of trust.

Mind-mindedness

Bowlby's view of what was necessary for sensitive care relied on the caregiver thinking about the thoughts and feelings of the child, and over time enabling the child to think about their own thoughts and feelings and the thoughts and feelings of the caregiver and other adults and children. This builds into an ability to make connections between feelings and behaviour in self and others – the capacity to mentalise. This ability in the child is strongly related to resilience, as it is only when a child is able to mentalise that they are able to make sense of themselves, their experiences and their relationships and be able to face new experiences and relationships with confidence.

Modern attachment researchers have built on the foundations of Bowlby's thinking. Elizabeth Meins and her colleagues have shown the importance for secure attachment and social development of what she calls the caregiver's "mind-mindedness" – the capacity to be interested in what the child is thinking and feeling, to see things from the *child's point of view,* and to *communicate this to the child* (Meins *et al*, 2003).

This process begins in infancy, with the sensitive caregiver viewing even the tiny baby as having thoughts and feelings that need to be understood. The caregiver speculates about these thoughts and feelings and reflects them back to the baby ('Are you hungry?' 'Were you feeling lonely?'). In doing so, the baby begins to understand and make sense of his inner experiences and feelings and gradually to manage and express them appropriately.

As the baby grows, the mind-minded caregiver also finds it natural to talk to the baby about their own feelings and behaviour ('Mummy's tired now, so we'll stop the game and have a drink') and that of others ('Your friend felt sad when you wouldn't share the toy, that's why she went off into the other room'). Through this sort of interaction and verbalisation of thoughts and feelings, the child learns to distinguish between different feelings in self and others, to express feelings in ways that are effective and socially acceptable, and to empathise with others.

David Howe (2011, p. 29) suggests: 'Parents who focus on their children's subjective experiences help them understand their own and other people's psychological states and how these are linked to actions and behaviour.' This builds the child's capacity to mentalise, to understand the links between mental states and behaviour.

Attachment and resilience

Many of the qualities that we associate with sensitive caregiving and secure attachment, and which are central to Secure Base, have strong links to the theory of resilience.

For a child, becoming resilient means developing the capacity not only to overcome past adversities, but to face future challenges with hope, confidence and competence. This may mean facing the ordinary challenges of starting a new school or not being picked for the football team. For adopted and fostered children, it may include facing more complex cognitive and emotional tasks, such as managing contact with birth relatives or coming to terms with a troubling life story.

Factors that are linked to resilience, such as trust in other people for support, positive self-esteem, self-efficacy and the capacity to reflect on your feelings and the feelings of others, are also associated with security of attachment. It is important to note that resilience, like a sense of security, can be promoted by the quality of caregiving a child receives.

The impact of abuse and neglect

Because most children who are fostered or adopted from care have experienced harmful parenting, it is important for caregivers to understand the impact of abuse and neglect on children's thinking, behaviour and development.

Where infants and children have not experienced the kind of sensitive parenting that promotes security and resilience – and instead have experienced parenting that was a source of fear – they will find it difficult to trust and will struggle to manage their feelings and behaviour. They are therefore likely to react negatively to offers of care and concern from foster carers and adoptive parents and may recreate in their new families cycles of negative behaviour that lead to them being rejected again (Crittenden, 1995). Children have adopted behaviours that helped them to survive when anxious and afraid, but these strategies bring additional difficulties in new families, which need to be managed with sensitivity and patience.

Secure and insecure attachment patterns

Attachment patterns are ways of thinking and behavioural strategies that children develop in order to feel safe and to maximise their opportunities for receiving protection and care from significant adults.

Different attachment patterns emerge in response to different types of caregiving. Ainsworth (1971) used a combination of home-based observations of caregiving in infancy and a laboratory situation called the Strange Situation to identify secure and two insecure (avoidant and ambivalent) attachment patterns. The Strange Situation involves the infant (12–18 months old) experiencing a series of brief separations and reunions with a primary caregiver while their reactions are observed, recorded and then analysed. Later research by Main and Solomon (1986) into those cases where the infant's recorded behaviour could not be explained using the existing three patterns, identified a third insecure attachment pattern – disorganised attachment.

Below, each of these four patterns is described in relation to the caregiving approach associated with it.

Secure attachment patterns

Secure attachment occurs when the infant or child is cared for by available, sensitive and responsive caregivers, who are accepting and co-operative, promoting trust and competence. When this care is predictable and mind-minded, the child over time becomes able to think about and manage thoughts, feelings and behaviour in order to become competent and successful in activities and relationships outside the family. In later adolescence and adulthood, this pattern is referred to as *autonomous* or *free to evaluate*, because of the importance of being able to think and to regulate emotions before acting.

Avoidant attachment patterns

When the caregiver finds it difficult to accept or respond sensitively to the infant's needs, the infant may find that their demands are rejected, and their feelings minimised and that the caregiver tries to take over in an intrusive, insensitive way. Although the rejecting caregiver's overall role in providing practical care and protection continues, the infant learns to shut down on their feelings in order to avoid upsetting the caregiver and provoking rejection or intrusion. It is safer and more comfortable to be self-reliant and undemanding and this also makes it more likely that the caregiver will stay close. The child is not avoiding a relationship, but avoiding showing feelings, particularly negative feelings, in order to maintain some kind of proximity and relationship. In later adolescence and adulthood, this pattern of minimising and defensively devaluing feelings and the significance of relationships is referred to as *dismissing*. As in infancy, the need for closeness and relationships continues but cannot be appropriately expressed or managed.

Ambivalent attachment patterns

In contrast, where the caregiver responds to the infant's demands, but only in a sporadic and unpredictable way that is insensitive to the child's signals, the infant finds it difficult to achieve proximity in a reliable way. Care and protection are sometimes available, but the caregiving is *uncertain* and *ineffective*. Initially, the infant may simply make demands almost constantly to attract and keep the attention of the caregiver or may become rather helpless in the absence of a predictably successful strategy. Over time, the infant tends to become needy and angry, a "clingy" but distrustful and *resistant* child. In later adolescence and adulthood, this pattern is referred to as *preoccupied* and *enmeshed,* but preoccupation with relationships and the need to be loved can be observed even in very young children who lack trust.

Disorganised attachment patterns

Where the caregiver is rejecting, unpredictable *and* frightening or frightened, the infant is caught in a dilemma of 'fear without solution' (Main and Hesse, 1990). Caregivers abdicate the caregiving role, experiencing themselves as out of control and become *hostile/helpless* to protect the child. The infant's drive to approach the caregiver for care and protection results in fear and increased rather than decreased anxiety. The absence of a possible strategy to achieve comfortable proximity in infancy leads to confused and disorganised behaviours. But over time the pre-school child starts to develop controlling behaviours to enable them to feel some degree of predictability and safety. These controlling behaviours usually include role-reversal in which a child acts towards others like a parent might towards a child, e.g. punitively aggressive, compulsively caregiving or compulsively self-reliant, i.e. not accepting care. However, feelings of anxiety and fear remain unresolved and reappear in sometimes chaotic and destructive forms at times of stress. In later adolescence and adulthood, this pattern is referred to as *unresolved*, reflecting the fact that experiences of loss, trauma or fear continue to trouble the adult mind.

Although many children who have been maltreated are likely to have disorganised patterns of attachment, not all children who are disorganised will have been maltreated. A caregiver may have experienced unresolved loss and trauma in the past. This may make the parent a source of anxiety rather than comfort for the infant, but does not mean that the parent is necessarily neglectful or abusive. However, the child may develop difficulties in their capacity to manage their emotions, their relationships and their behaviour.

The importance of a secure base

What happens when children do not have a secure base?

Early experiences of separation or neglectful or abusive parenting will cause children to remain anxious and to distrust close relationships. Children adapt to the lack of a secure base by developing different patterns of behaviour. For instance, they may become wary and defended (avoidant) or especially needy and demanding of care and attention (ambivalent). Children who have experienced unpredictable or frightening care may try to make their environment more predictable through role-reversing and controlling behaviour (disorganised). These behaviours are characteristic of insecure attachment patterns and indicate an absence of a secure base.

What happens when children are removed from a harmful family environment?

For many children, serious experiences of neglect and maltreatment will have had a profound effect. They will have developed negative expectations of adults and themselves as part of their internal working model of relationships. They will transfer these expectations into new environments (such as foster or adoptive families), along with the patterns of defensive behaviour that have functioned as survival strategies in the past. In these circumstances, children will find it hard to let adults come close enough to establish trusting relationships and provide a secure base. The risk, then, is that feelings and behaviours might become fixed in destructive cycles and the damage of the past will not be healed.

What can be done to help?

Attachment theory would suggest that exposure to warm, consistent and reliable caregiving can change children's previous expectations, both of close adults and of themselves and there is ample evidence from research and practice to support this (Wilson *et al*, 2003; Beek and Schofield, 2004; Cairns, 2004; Schofield and Beek, 2009; Howe, 2011).

The role of adults who can provide secure base caregiving, therefore, is of central importance. They must take on a parenting/caregiving role for the child, but they must also become a *therapeutic* caregiver in order to change the child's most fundamental sense of self and others (internal working model).

In order to achieve this, they must care for the child in ways that demonstrate, implicitly and explicitly, to the child that they are trustworthy and reliable, physically and emotionally available and sensitive to his needs. In addition, they must be mindful of the protective strategies that the child has learned in order to feel safe in the past and adjust their approaches so that their parenting feels comfortable and acceptable to the child rather than undermining or threatening.

The ensuing relationships will provide a secure base, from which children can develop and be supported to explore and maximise their potential. Achieving this outcome is the goal of the Secure Base model.

What may be the impact on caregivers of providing a secure base to troubled children?

There is no doubt that although offering therapeutic care that changes how troubled children feel about themselves and relate to other people is very rewarding, it is also a very emotionally demanding role. Children who have had to survive frightening environments in the past may have adopted behaviours that can alarm and overwhelm caregivers. Foster and adoptive caregivers need support from their own networks and from professionals to be able to maintain their patience, sensitivity and commitment to the child, even in the face of initial anger and rejection by the child.

Do adults/caregivers also need a secure base?

Yes. As we move through the lifespan, we form new attachment relationships with friends and partners. These relationships serve the same function for adults as they do for children: they provide a secure base which offers comfort and reassurance and, at the same time, allows us to operate in the world with confidence. In the words of Bowlby:

> *All of us, from the cradle to the grave, are happiest when life is organised as a series of excursions, long or short, from the secure base provided by our attachment figures.*
> (Bowlby, 1988, p. 62)

3 Secure Base

Secure Base provides a positive framework for therapeutic caregiving that helps infants, children and young people to move towards greater security and which builds resilience. It focuses on the interactions that occur between caregivers and children on a day-to-day, minute-by-minute basis in the family environment. But it also considers how those relationships can enable the child to develop competence in the outside world of school, peer group and community.

The caregiving cycle

It can be helpful, first, to think about caregiver–child interactions as having the potential to shape the thinking and feeling and ultimately the behaviour of the child. This caregiving cycle begins with the child's needs and behaviour and then focuses on what is going on in the mind of the caregiver. How a caregiver *thinks and feels* about a child's needs and behaviour will determine his or her *caregiving behaviours*. The caregiver may draw on their own ideas about what children need or what makes a good parent and, for foster carers and adopters, from what they have learned in training.

The resulting caregiving behaviours convey certain messages to the child. The child's *thinking and feeling* about himself and other people will be affected by these messages and there will be a consequent impact on his *development*. We have chosen to represent this process in a circular model, the caregiving cycle, which shows the interconnectedness of caregiver–child relationships, minds and behaviour, as well as their ongoing potential for movement and change.

Figure 1 **The caregiving cycle**

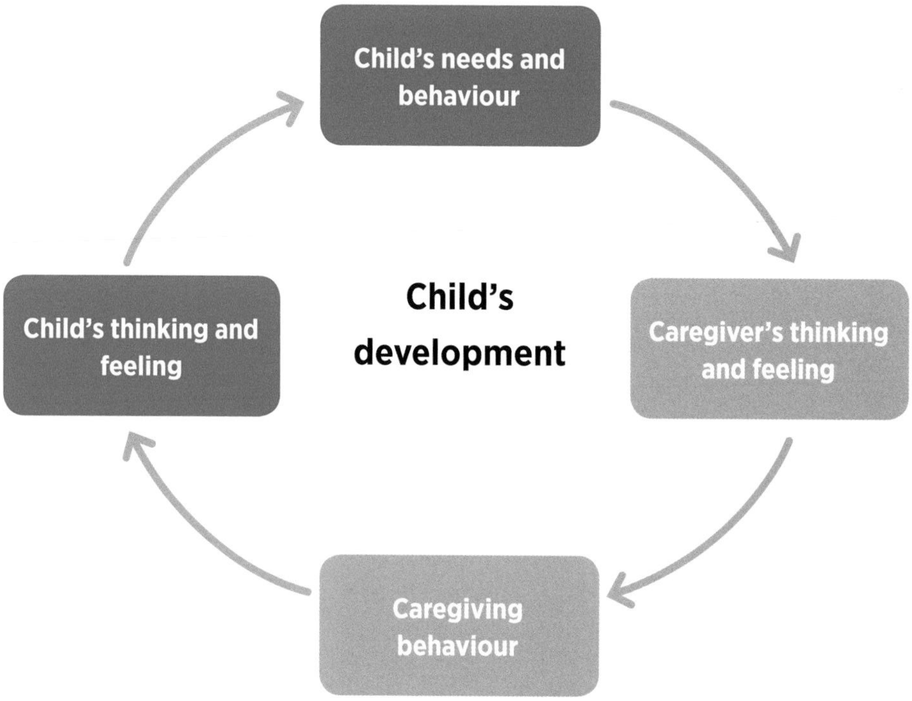

This caregiving cycle encompasses the many interactions of family life. These range from the moment to moment exchanges over breakfast to managing major emotional or behavioural crises. Each interaction conveys a number of messages to the child and has an incremental effect on the child's beliefs about himself, beliefs about other people and the relationship between self and others. These internal working models will influence the child's functioning and development. So how well this caregiving cycle supports the child to think and feel about himself and other people with trust and confidence will make a significant difference.

Dimensions of caregiving

For Secure Base, we have used five dimensions of caregiving. The first four dimensions are drawn from attachment theory as set out by Bowlby (1969) and Ainsworth (1971, 1978) and associated with secure attachment. We have added to the model an additional dimension, family membership, that is relevant for all children but can be particularly challenging for children who are separated from their families of origin.

Each of the five caregiving dimensions is associated with a particular developmental benefit for the child:

Caregiving dimension	Developmental benefit
Availability	Helping the child to trust
Sensitivity	Helping the child to manage feelings
Acceptance	Building the child's self-esteem
Co-operation	Helping the child to feel effective
Family membership	Helping the child to belong

It is important to bear in mind that these dimensions are not entirely distinct from each other. In the real world of caregiving behaviour, they overlap and combine. For example, a caregiver who is playing with a child in a focused, child-led way may be doing so with sensitivity and acceptance as well as demonstrating availability and promoting co-operation. Similarly, it is difficult for a caregiver to be sensitive without also being emotionally available – or for a child to experience a sense of family membership if he does not feel accepted, or to feel effective if he does not have a reasonable level of self-esteem. However, each dimension does need to be thought about separately as this allows us to focus specifically on certain strengths and difficulties in the child and the caregiver. For instance, a caregiver may be more or less available in certain circumstances or for certain children.

To illustrate the importance of the interactions between each of the caregiving dimensions and the developmental dimensions, they have been represented as a star-shaped model (Figure 2). This has the benefit for foster carers, adopters and practitioners of providing a simple but powerful, positive and memorable image that can be directly used as a focus for discussion and for working together to promote the child's well-being and happiness.

Secure Base therefore provides a framework for caregivers and for those who support them to think in more detail about the different but connected caregiving approaches that can help a child to move towards greater security and resilience. It is a positive, strengths-based approach that focuses on how the many interactions between the caregiver and the child in the course of a day provide opportunities for positive change. But it also considers how close relationships and positive interactions can enable the child to relate to the wider circle of family and friends, and to develop competence in the outside world.

Each dimension is discussed in turn, using the caregiving cycle, to provide the framework for making sense of what caregivers and children think, feel and do and for understanding what can lead to upward or downward spirals in their relationship and in the child's development, from infancy to adolescence.

For each dimension, a range of caregiving approaches are suggested. It is important to choose approaches that take into account the chronological and emotional age of the child and to try approaches and activities that this particular child is likely to accept, enjoy and benefit from. If one approach doesn't quite work, others may be more successful. These suggestions are just a starting point – foster carers and adoptive parents need encouragement to be creative in thinking about what may be helpful to their particular child at this stage in her development.

Figure 2 **The Secure Base Model**

AVAILABILITY – helping the child to trust

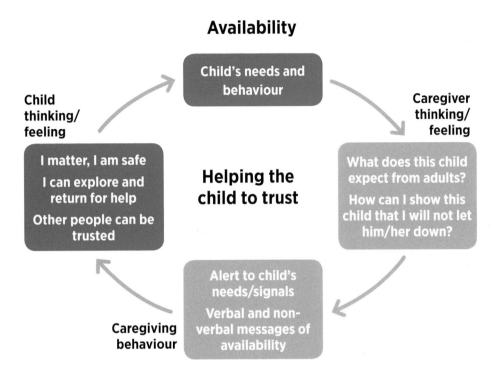

Availability

Child's needs and behaviour

Child thinking/ feeling

I matter, I am safe

I can explore and return for help

Other people can be trusted

Helping the child to trust

Caregiver thinking/ feeling

What does this child expect from adults?

How can I show this child that I will not let him/her down?

Caregiving behaviour

Alert to child's needs/signals

Verbal and non-verbal messages of availability

This dimension focuses on the caregiver's ability to convey a strong sense of being physically and emotionally **available** to meet the child's needs, both when they are together and when they are apart. When the caregiver can do this, the child begins to **trust** that her needs will be met warmly, consistently and reliably. Anxiety is reduced and the child gains the confidence to explore the world, safe in the knowledge that care and protection are there if needed.

The child's needs and behaviour

Most children who come into foster care and adoption, from infancy to adolescence, have lacked available care and protection from birth family caregivers. They have often experienced parents who have reacted to the child's needs with frustration, anxiety and rejection, or have "blown hot and cold" according to their own needs and preoccupations. Each of these reactions from parents will cause children to have anxieties and uncertainties around caregiving and their own safety and security. They will find it hard to trust that an adult will always be available or that their needs will be met consistently, safely and kindly. Most detrimentally, parents may have reacted to a needy child with unpredictable anger or frightening aggression, causing the child to feel deep fear, panic, confusion and helplessness. The child is then likely to associate closeness with feelings of fear and dread and feel panicked by the approach of any potential caregiver, however trustworthy they may be.

These deeply rooted experiences may lead children either to distance themselves from their new caregivers, to clamour constantly for their attention, to feel helpless, or to be determinedly in control. These defensive strategies, associated with insecure attachment, which were necessary for survival at an earlier stage, can become problematic, stressful or hurtful to new caregivers who want so much to nurture, soothe and protect children from further harm.

Caregiver thinking and feeling

The challenge for new caregivers is a complex one. The eventual goal is to change the children's expectations of adults – to convince children that they *can* rely on adults to care for them and meet their needs. Firstly, however, they may have to disentangle some confusing messages. Through words and behaviour, children may be indicating 'I don't need you, I prefer to look after myself', or 'I need you all the time, but can never be satisfied by you', or 'I can only manage my anxiety by controlling you and everything that happens in the household'.

New caregivers may have to remind themselves of the true needs that lie behind these messages and this is no easy task when they are accompanied by extremely resistant, needy or hostile behaviour. Caregivers may need additional support, therefore, to help them to *think* about this particular child's previous experiences and speculate on **what does *this* child expect from adults?** In the light of this, the caregiver can think in a more focused way about the question, **How can I show *this* child that I will not let her down?** Trust-building interventions can then be targeted more precisely.

Caregiving behaviour

With this in mind, caregivers can begin to be more **alert to their child's needs and signals** and then take opportunities to do and say things that will begin to change the child's expectations of herself and adults. They will give **verbal and non-verbal messages of availability**. But – and this perhaps, is the greatest skill of secure base caregiving – they will find ways of doing this that feel comfortable and acceptable to the individual child, such as knowing when to move closer and when to wait for a child to make the first move herself. Also important is the capacity of the caregiver to generate *flexible theories* about what is going on for the child (e.g. this behaviour may be caused by a bad experience in early childhood, a difficult day at school or both), to try different approaches and to wait patiently for small changes.

The child's thinking and feeling

As children begin to *trust* that close adults are not going to disappear or let them down, their thinking will begin to change in subtle ways. They will begin to gain a sense of **I matter, I am safe, I can explore and return to my secure base for help,** and, crucially, **other people can be trusted.**

As anxiety is diminished, the drive to explore, learn and play becomes greater. There will be greater confidence and competence to venture away from the secure base and discover the wider world – but there will also be an increasing capacity to rely on caregivers for comfort and nurture and to enjoy appropriate closeness. Signs of progress in these areas may be slow to appear, but they are among the most exciting and rewarding for caregivers to observe.

CAREGIVING APPROACHES FOR HELPING THE CHILD TO BUILD TRUST

Day-to-day caregiving

- Establish predictable routines around mealtimes, getting up and going to bed. Make these explicit to the child and talk them through in advance.

- Use a calendar or picture chart to help the child predict and anticipate events.

- Ensure that the child feels specially cared for and nurtured when ill, hurt or sad.

- Be unobtrusively available if the child is anxious but finds it hard to talk or accept comfort (for example, sit nearby, suggest a ride in the car).

- Offer verbal and non-verbal support for safe exploration.

- Respond promptly to the child's signals for support or comfort or reassure an older child that you will respond as promised as soon as possible. For example: 'I must quickly finish what I am doing and then I will come and help you straight away'.

Building trust when caregiver and child are apart

- Manage separations carefully, with open communication about why it is happening, how long it will be, and clear "goodbyes" and "hellos".

- Ensure that the child always knows how to contact you when you are apart.

- Allow the child to take a small item or photo from home to school.

- Use your mobile phone to ring or text to help the child know that you are thinking of her.

- Place a small surprise on the child's bed when she is at school. Tell her that you have done this because you have thought about her during the day.

- Keep a "goodies tub" in the kitchen and put small treats in it for the child to have in the evening. Tell her that you have done this because you have thought about her during the day.

Games and activities

- Ask the child to draw a fortress or make one in clay or sand. The child may choose miniature toys or animals to stand for the main people in her life. Ask the child to show and talk about which ones she would let into her fort and which ones she would keep out and why (from Sunderland, 2000).

- Ask the child to draw a bridge with themselves on one side and someone they trust on the other. Ask her to draw a speech bubble coming out of their mouth and write in it what they are thinking or saying. Do the same with the other person (from Sunderland, 2000).

- Hand-holding games such as "ring a roses" or clapping games.

- Reading stories with the child on your lap or sitting close.

- Leading each other blindfold.

- Three-legged race, bat and ball.

- Throwing a ball or beanbag to each other.

- Blowing and chasing bubbles together.

- Rocking, singing, gently holding the child.

- Face painting; rubbing lotion onto each other's hands and arms.

- Brushing and plaiting hair, painting nails.

- Teaching a new skill or learning one together.

SENSITIVITY – helping the child to manage feelings

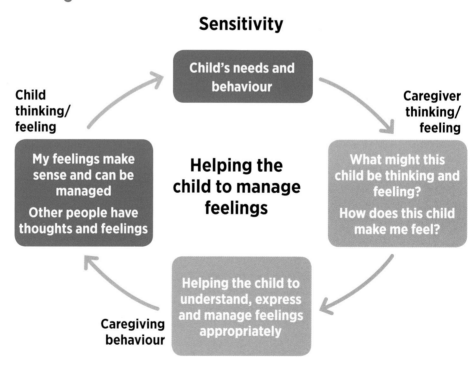

Sensitivity refers to the caregiver's capacity to "stand in the shoes" of the child, to think flexibly about what the child may be thinking and feeling and to reflect this back to the child. The sensitive caregiver also thinks about their own feelings and shares them appropriately with the child. The child thus learns to think about and value his own ideas and feelings and the thoughts and feelings of others and is helped to reflect on, organise and manage his own feelings. This capacity to reflect on, manage and regulate feelings then enables the child to reflect on, manage and regulate his behaviour.

The child's needs and behaviour

Children from difficult backgrounds have mostly lacked opportunities to have their thoughts and feelings acknowledged and understood – this can be true for children from infancy to adolescence. They may have been in situations where there was no one able or available to help them deal with strong feelings, so panic, anger or despair may have overwhelmed them at times. Or they may have had caregivers who denied or mis-labelled their feelings, distorting their sense of reality to the point where they could not discern the "truth" of what they felt in any situation. A child may have accidentally knocked over an ornament and be very upset about the harm caused, but be told that he had done this deliberately to upset his mother and that he didn't care. Sometimes, children will have been cared for by adults who could not manage and regulate their own feelings and children may have been blamed or feel themselves to blame for chaos or violence in the household. For a range of reasons, previous caregivers may have been too anxiously absorbed with their own distress or too preoccupied with their own needs to attune themselves to the minds and feelings of their children.

Lacking the resource of a safe and containing adult mind or a supportive scaffolding for managing their feelings, children develop their own ways of coping with them. This might involve expressing their feelings excessively, using feelings to control others, holding feelings in or denying that they exist at all. Each strategy is problematic in a foster or adoptive family setting, where feelings need to be communicated fairly openly, in a managed and regulated way, in order to build trusting relationships.

Caregiver thinking and feeling

For new caregivers, a primary task is to reflect on and make sense of their children's feelings and how they are reflected in their behaviour. They must attempt to tune in to their child, stand in the child's shoes and try to imagine – **what might this child be thinking and feeling?** They need to be particularly thoughtful about the child's previous experiences and flexible in their thinking about how these might have shaped his thinking processes and expression of feelings. Although it is painful to do so, the capacity to project oneself into the mind of a child who has been maltreated is important. It is from this starting point that caregivers can begin to think about the child's beliefs and expectations of himself and others and to reflect on how this might connect with his current behaviours.

The caregiver's thinking will not only be about what is in the child's mind about the present and the past – it will also be about making sense of the way in which the child reacts to small daily events. But the darkness of aspects of the child's history and the impact of the child's anxiety and dysregulated feelings on carers can, if not fully understood, disturb the mind of the caregiver or the cheerful and positive atmosphere of the household. In this context, there is really no substitute for a containing relationship with a thoughtful, reflective social worker, who can bear the pain and cope with the complexity of thinking about the child's history and current behaviours accurately, without distortion and without being overwhelmed, and who can allow the caregiver to reflect honestly on the question, **how does this child make me feel?**

Caregiving behaviour

With this supportive framework in place, caregivers can begin to adopt a range of approaches geared towards helping children to **understand and express their feelings appropriately**. An important first stage is that of *naming feelings*, helping the child to reflect on them, recognise them and think about their origin. Often, the expression of feelings is either suppressed or excessive and caregivers must help some children to show feelings more freely and others to contain and moderate them. In order to help children to understand and respond to the feelings of others, caregivers need to feel comfortable in expressing and discussing the full range of their own feelings. In particular, they can show children that *mixed feelings* are "normal" and that combinations of love and anger, longing and distrust, anxiety and eager anticipation are part of the human condition – affecting not only them but also their birth parents, foster carers, adoptive parents, friends and social workers.

The child's thinking and feeling

The emotional education provided by sensitive caregivers enables the child to discover that **my feelings make sense** and **I can manage my feelings,** gaining confidence that feelings will not become overwhelming to himself or others. Finally, the child can be helped to understand that **other people have thoughts and feelings** that must also be taken into account.

As the child's thinking shifts and develops in these important ways, feelings are better regulated, and there is a likelihood of more constructive relationships, greater empathy and more pro-social than antisocial behaviour.

CAREGIVING APPROACHES FOR HELPING THE CHILD TO MANAGE FEELINGS

Day-to-day caregiving

- Observe the child carefully – keep a diary, note patterns, the unexpected, try to stand in the child's shoes. Gently feed back observations to the child, as appropriate.

- Anticipate what will cause confusion and distress for the child and avoid if possible.

- Express interest, at a level that is comfortable for the child, in his thoughts and feelings.

- Provide shared, pleasurable activity and a "commentary" on the feelings experienced by yourself and the child.

- Encourage the child to *stop* and *think* before reacting.

- Help the child recover/repair the situation/make things better after losing control of his feelings – praise him for doing this.

- Name and talk about feelings in everyday situations, e.g. 'Your friend is going on holiday tomorrow. I wonder how he is feeling?'.

- Reflect on events and relationships – discuss mixed feelings and feelings that change over time.

Games and activities

- Make a "My calendar" to help the child to see and remember/anticipate what will happen each day.

- Play "sensory" games (involving touch, sound, smell, observation).

- Use clay, paint or crayons to help the child to express feelings.

- Use play to help the child to make sense of the world, how things work, cause and effect.

- Use stories or puppets to develop empathy in the child – 'Poor owl, how does he feel now his tree has been cut down?', etc.

- Use television programmes/films to help the child to focus on why people feel different things and how they can feel different things at the same time.

- Collect tickets, pictures, leaflets, stickers, etc, and discuss with a child their feelings about each event.

- Make an "experiences book" to help children remember and reflect on positive events, and to understand the passage of time – past, present and anticipated future.

ACCEPTANCE – building the child's self-esteem

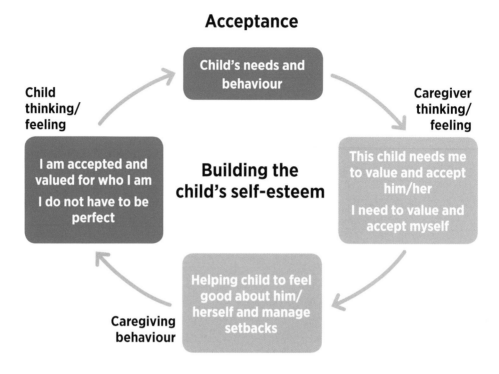

Acceptance

Acceptance is a necessary part of secure caregiving. This dimension describes the ways in which the caregiver is able to convey that the child is unconditionally accepted and valued for who she is, for her difficulties as well as her strengths. This forms the foundation of positive self-esteem – the child feels good about herself. She can experience herself as worthy of receiving love, help and support and also as robust and able to deal with setbacks and adversity. This both reinforces a positive internal working model and builds resilience.

This area of caregiving builds on the dimensions of *availability* and *sensitivity*. Children need to learn to **trust** and to **manage their feelings** in order to believe the praise of caregivers and to take up opportunities that are on offer. But building a child's self-esteem through activities can also build and reinforce trust and help a child to manage anxiety and express both positive and negative feelings more freely.

The child's needs and behaviour

Many children who come into foster care and adoption have a profound sense of worthlessness and low self-esteem, often complex and deep-rooted in origin. Their early parenting may have lacked warmth and acceptance. For some children, family life may have been frightening at times and the tendency for young children to see themselves as having some responsibility for negative events can lead them to experience themselves as dangerous, bad and worthy only of rejection or punishment.

Low self-esteem for children may also be connected with multiple separations and losses of familiar people and, for some children, may be compounded by the stigma and sense of difference incurred by being fostered or adopted. Children, therefore, are likely to have deep-seated doubts about their fundamental goodness, whether or not they deserve loving care and whether or not they will receive it if they are "naughty" or needy.

Children who do not have an internal working model of close adults as warm and accepting, and themselves as loved and loveable, will find it hard to face the world with confidence. They have not learned that they can be both "good and bad" at different times, "clever or not so clever", and yet still be accepted and valued. They often believe that if they cannot be the best, then they must be the worst. The danger, then, is that a child becomes trapped in a negative cycle expecting failure or rejection and behaving in ways (anxiously or aggressively) that are likely to produce this outcome.

Caregiver thinking and feeling

Caregivers must hold in mind the sense that **this child needs me to value and accept her**, whatever the stresses of caring for the child may be. Alongside this, and especially if caring for the child is challenging, the caregiver must remember that **I need to value and accept myself**, so that their own emotional resources do not become depleted. This may be a key area of intervention for support workers. Caregivers who are feeling overwhelmed by their child's needs may need to be reminded of their strengths and skills and that it is the child's history that is creating problems in the family, rather than their own shortcomings as caregivers.

Caregivers need to have a belief in the child as special and be able to develop hopefulness about her potential. Schofield *et al* (2000) found that successful caregivers invariably were able to express this belief, in spite of a child's difficulties, e.g. 'Very hard work…but he's got the potential to be a really nice young man'; 'She's an absolute rogue. And you would never want that squashed. It's lovely. It's just got to be channelled' (pp. 198–9).

By modelling acceptance of both strengths and difficulties in the caregiver, support workers can also convey the message, 'You do not have to be perfect', alongside providing caregivers with advice, discussion and training that will help them to develop new approaches and to parent more positively.

Caregiving behaviour

Caregivers can then build a range of skills and strategies for **helping the child to feel good about herself and to manage setbacks**. Difficult behaviour can be approached in ways that do not undermine the caregiver's own self-esteem or that of the child. The positive message to the child is: 'Nobody is good at everything but everybody is good at something', and so there is a focus on activities and interactions that both help caregivers to regain their sense of being competent and successful and enable children to feel positive about themselves.

This positive approach does not mean that behaviour difficulties are not challenged or that goals are not set to reduce behaviours that are upsetting or antisocial. On the contrary, it is critical for children, especially older children, to feel acceptable and accepted not only in the family, but also in their peer group and the wider community. Caregivers, therefore, have to manage a careful balance between accepting children as they are *and* helping them to change aspects of behaviour that threaten their acceptance by others.

The child's thinking and feeling

The goal is for children to begin to think: **I am accepted and valued for who I am. I do not have to be perfect in order to be loved and valued**.

For some children, feeling good about and accepting themselves will always prove difficult, even with the most sensitive and accepting care. But self-esteem is so critical to healthy development that even small degrees of progress are worth working for.

CAREGIVING APPROACHES FOR BUILDING THE CHILD'S SELF-ESTEEM

Day-to-day caregiving

- Praise the child for achieving small tasks and responsibilities.
- Provide toys and games that create a sense of achievement.
- Liaise closely with the child's nursery or school to ensure a sense of achievement.
- Use positive language. For example, 'Hold the cup tight – good, well done', rather than 'Don't drop the cup'.
- Offer the child a brief explanation of why behaviour is not acceptable and a clear indication of what is preferred. For example: 'If you shout it's really hard for me to hear what you want to say. I want to be able to hear you, so please talk in an ordinary voice.'
- Use dolls, toys, games and books that promote a positive sense of the child's ethnic, religious and cultural background.
- Ensure that the child's ethnic, religious and cultural background is valued and celebrated within the household.
- Model the acceptance of difference in words and behaviour.
- Model a sense of pride in self and surroundings.
- Model within the family that it is OK not to be perfect, that 'no one is good at everything but everyone is good at something'.

Games and activities

- Help the child to list and think about all the things she has done that she feels proud of. Use photos and other mementos to record these events.

- List, alongside the child, all the things that make you feel proud of her. This can include acceptance of her limitations (e.g. a time when the child tried but did not succeed at something, was able to accept losing, etc).

- Encourage the child to draw, paint, make a clay model or play music to express how it feels when she feels good about herself. Do the same for yourself.

- As a family group, suggest that each person in the family writes down one good thing about all other family members, so that each child gets given a set of positive things about themselves.

- Make a poster with the child of "best achievements".

- Ask the child to teach you something that she is good at – such as a computer game or a joke.

- Discover and support activities and interests that the child enjoys and can be successful in. This may need active support (liaison with club leader, becoming a helper at the club, etc).

- Play rule-based games with the child, such as board games – help the child to manage feelings/enjoy the competition, whether winning or losing.

- With the child, draw a picture of the child – encourage the child to make positive statements about different parts of herself – shiny hair, pretty T-shirt, friendly smiles, feet good at kicking a ball – help the child to write them on the drawing and talk about them.

CO-OPERATION – helping the child to feel effective

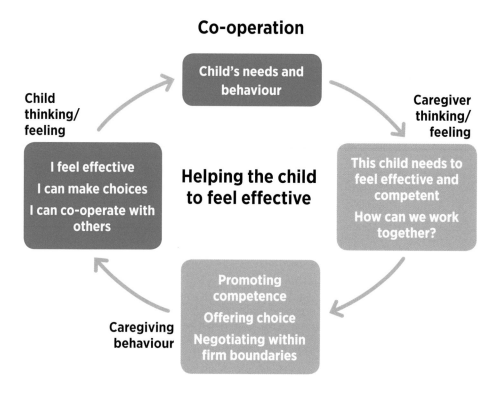

Co-operation is a key goal of a successful caregiving relationship. Within this dimension, the caregiver thinks about the child as an autonomous individual whose wishes, feelings and goals are valid and meaningful and who needs to feel effective. The caregiver therefore looks for ways of promoting autonomy, but also working together and achieving co-operation with the child wherever possible. This helps the child to feel more effective and competent, to feel confident in turning to others for help when necessary, and to be able to compromise and co-operate.

The child's needs and behaviour

Fostered and adopted children have seldom experienced this co-operative approach to parenting as part of their early care. Birth parents who were struggling with their own needs may have been over-controlling and intrusive, denying children the opportunity to make choices, to feel competent and be effective. Parents may have lacked the skills or capacity to negotiate, resulting in interventions that were harsh and abrupt or weak and ineffective. Additionally, in stressed and disadvantaged households there are often fewer opportunities for play, fun and mutually enjoyable activities.

For a range of reasons, therefore, children may not have developed a sense of themselves as competent individuals, nor of adults as co-operative partners, either in exploration and play or in managing difficulties. As a result, they may become passive and over-compliant in their relationships with adults or they may seek excessive control and influence over them.

Caregiver thinking and feeling

Most caregivers would agree that all children need to feel effective and competent and they will know that most children enjoy and benefit from opportunities to act on their environment, make choices and take gradual steps towards independence. But children who feel ineffective and who have lacked appropriate control and influence in their lives can behave in ways that trigger difficult feelings and painful associations in their caregivers, making it harder for them to work towards these goals.

In most cases, therefore, caregivers may need help in taking a step back to consider: 'How is this child affecting my sense of effectiveness and competence?' Understanding your own experiences and the extent to which you need to be in control or are finding it hard to take control can be an important first step in co-operative caregiving. Shared thinking about the child's earlier experiences of caregiving and the ways in which issues of competence and control might have been handled with the child in the past can also be helpful for the caregiver. This leads to a stronger position from which to address the questions: **How can I help this child to feel more effective and competent?** and **How can we work together?** The caregiver is then able to take a step back, and think in terms of forming a co-operative partnership with the child in order to achieve their shared and separate goals.

Caregiving behaviour

In co-operative caregiving, there are two important areas of "additional" parenting activity. The first is to help children to learn that it can be safe and rewarding to be active in completing tasks, solving problems for themselves, and making choices. To achieve this, caregivers will need to actively structure an environment that **promotes competence** and **offers choice**, providing opportunities for their children to feel genuinely effective. At all times, sensitive caregivers must be mindful of the delicate balance between facilitating appropriate dependency and promoting appropriate independence.

The second task for caregivers is to help children to experience co-operative relationships in which each partner contributes to the other's goals. This involves making co-operation enjoyable, actively demonstrating that sharing and working together can be rewarding and fun. At the same time, **negotiating within firm boundaries** ensures that safe and reasonable limits are set and comfortable compromises can be reached when necessary.

The child's thinking and feeling

The caregiver must bear in mind that the child will need to have a developing trust in a secure base before he can feel safe enough to tackle a difficult task or make new choices. Only when the foundations of trust are in place will the child be able to take the risk of thinking and behaving differently, being assertive but also co-operative.

Experiences of becoming increasingly competent to solve problems, to approach challenges and to **make choices** will help the child to **feel more effective**. And positive experiences of working together with trusted adults will develop the sense that it is rewarding to **compromise and co-operate**.

CAREGIVING APPROACHES FOR HELPING CHILDREN TO FEEL EFFECTIVE

Day-to-day caregiving

- Within the house and garden, minimise hazards and things that the child cannot touch and keep "out of bounds" areas secure so that the child can explore without adult "interference" when he is ready to do so.

- Make opportunities for choices. For example, allow the child to choose the cereal at the supermarket, a pudding for a family meal, or what to wear for a certain activity.

- Ensure that daily routines include time to relax together and share a pleasurable activity.

- Do not try to tackle several problem areas at any one time. Set one or two priorities and work on them gradually until there are sustained signs of progress. Ensure that these are acknowledged.

- Use co-operative language wherever possible. For example: 'Would you like to come and have a sandwich after you've washed your hands?', rather than 'Wash your hands before you eat your sandwich'.

Games and activities

- Suggest small tasks and responsibilities within the child's capabilities. Ensure recognition and praise when achieved. If tasks become an issue, do them alongside the child – this is a chance to show availability.

- Introduce toys where the action of the child achieves a rewarding result, for example, pushing a button, touching or shaking something.

- Find shared activities that the child enjoys and that produce a clear result, for example, baking cakes.

- Introduce games that promote co-operation, turn-taking and teamwork.

- Seek opportunities for the child to co-operate with other children – you may need to be present so that this is managed successfully.

- Find time for interactions that promote working together, for example, simple action rhymes and songs, clapping games, ball and beanbag games, learning a dance together, building or making something together, a shared "adventure" or new experience.

- Help the child to identify a target that they would like to achieve, do, change, etc. Settle on one where something done now will make a difference. Discuss what the young person can do and negotiate simple, relevant and achievable steps that they can take. When agreed, draw a simple staircase and write one task on each of the steps of the staircase. For example, if the target is 'Go to see Manchester United play at home', steps might be: use the internet to find out dates of home games this season, settle on a suitable date and put on the calendar, find out train times, etc. Set a time to review progress and think about further steps needed.

FAMILY MEMBERSHIP – helping the child to belong

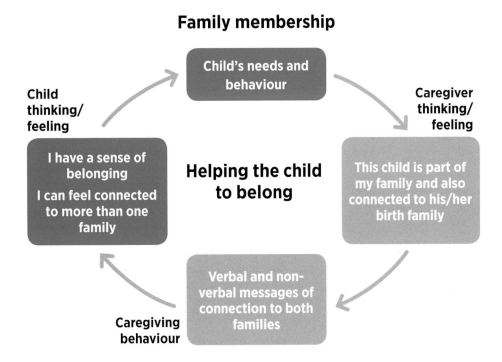

Family membership is a vital strand of healthy emotional and psychosocial development. A child who has no close family relationships will carry feelings of psychological and social dislocation. In contrast, the certainty of unconditional family membership can provide anchorage and the reassurance of practical and emotional support throughout life, acting as a psychosocial secure base for exploration, identity and personal development.

The family membership dimension refers to the capacity of the foster carer or adoptive parent to include the child, socially and personally, as a full family member, in ways that are appropriate to the longer-term plan for the child. At the same time, the caregiver must help the child to establish an appropriate sense of *connectedness* to her birth family. For children in short-term care with a plan to return home, the sense of connection to the birth family may be the dominant source of family membership and sense of belonging. In permanent placements, the long-term foster or adoptive family will be the primary source of membership and belonging, with the birth family role depending very much on the quality of the child's relationships with birth family members and the quality of any contact. But whatever the nature of the child's family connections to foster, adoptive or birth families, she will need both a sense of belonging and help to develop a coherent family narrative that makes sense to her at her particular age and stage.

The child's needs and behaviour

Each child separated from their birth family will bring a unique set of experiences of family life and each of these experiences will have shaped their expectations of the new environment and their sense of what it means to be a family member.

It is important to remember that, for most children, there will have been good times as well as difficult ones, positive memories as well as sad or frightening ones. For all children, the challenges of adapting to a new family life are enormous. Depending on their age and understanding, all children will be grappling with different degrees of loss (of people, places, pets and friends), uncertainty (How long will I stay? Do they really want me?) and anxiety (Will I be safe? Will I fit in?). The simple tasks of getting up in the morning and having breakfast in an unfamiliar setting can be mountains to climb for a child. It is hard to overestimate the potential stresses and strains that are involved in making the move to a new family, while managing feelings of loss and strong, although in some cases potentially harmful, ties to birth families.

Once the child begins to settle in the foster or adoptive family, these early messages of acceptance as part of the family will become consolidated so that she can feel reassured that she belongs. Even in those circumstances, where there is some uncertainty about the future plans for the child, full inclusion in the family routines and activities is an essential part of providing a secure base that reduces the child's anxiety and restores self-esteem.

Caregiver thinking and feeling

Caregivers will need to be aware that a child's sense of connection to the birth family and foster or adoptive families will vary according to the nature of the *plan* for the child and the *quality* of relationships in both the birth family and the new family.

For instance, a child who is to have a short stay in a foster family with a plan to return home will usually need a fairly close involvement with birth family members and events, but will also value being treated just the same as other family members. Children in long-term foster families will need and can be expected to be treated as full family members through to adulthood, even in the absence of legal parental responsibility for the carers. Most foster children will also have continuing contact with their birth family that has to be managed constructively. Adoption confers full legal membership of the new family, with support provided into adulthood, but adopted children need also to achieve a sense of connection with their birth families, whether through contact (where appropriate) and/or through open, reflective discussion within the adoptive family.

What is important in all cases, however, is the capacity of the foster or adoptive family to both welcome and absorb new members and also to be thoughtful, reflective and open towards the individual child and his or her birth family. The thinking is therefore complex since it involves holding a balance between two powerful and sometimes conflicting ideas: **this child is part of our family as well as connected to her birth family**.

Caregiving behaviour

For caregivers, the primary task is to provide an environment that is emotionally warm, physically comfortable, accepting, and supportive of its members and that sets clear but reasonable expectations for shared living as a member of the family. The variations in how family membership is communicated are enormous and span the full range of culture, class, language, social norms and religious practice. It is here that we see a clear link to attachment theory, since sensitive caregivers provide the sort of environment described above and yet also have the capacity to be *reflective* in relation to the child's needs and feelings about birth family membership.

Sensitive caregiving in this dimension therefore involves seeking opportunities to provide **verbal and non-verbal messages of connection to both families**. These must be sensitively adapted to the child's changing needs and circumstances, with the aim of helping the child to feel a coherent sense of identity in what may be a complex network of relationships.

The child's thinking and feeling

The combination of inclusion and recognition of having connections to more than one family can enhance the child's felt security – 'I am safe and secure in this family, but I can also think and talk about how I feel about my birth family.' Over time, this will allow children to process their complex feelings, recognise and express different and mixed feelings, and manage their dual or sometimes multiple family connections at a level that feels compatible with their particular circumstance, wishes and feelings. They can move towards a position where their thinking and behaviour reflect a coherent sense of self and acceptance that '**I belong**' and '**I can feel connected to more than one family**'.

CAREGIVING APPROACHES FOR HELPING CHILDREN TO BELONG

Belonging to the adoptive or foster family

- Explain to the child from the beginning how the family works – its routines and expectations, its choice of food and favourite television programmes – so that the child can see how to fit in.

- Adapt those routines where possible and reasonable to accommodate the child's norms and help the child feel at home, e.g. meal times or bedtime.

- Have special places for the child in the home, e.g. a hook for the child's coat, a place at the table, bedding and bedroom decoration (posters, etc) that reflect the child's age and interests.

- Promote family mealtimes and activities (e.g. going bowling) where the child can feel fully accepted as part of the family.

- Ensure that extended family members and friends welcome the child and treat the child as one of the family.

- Have photographs of the child on display – alongside photographs of other children in the family or who have lived in the family and moved on/grown up.

- Make an album of family experiences that have included the child. This can help the child to reflect on family life and, in a short-term placement, can be taken home to the birth family or to a new placement.

- Make sure the school knows (and the child knows that the school knows) that you are the family caring for the child and need to be kept informed of any concerns but also of achievements and events to celebrate.

- Talk about regular family activities that will include the child.

Being connected to the birth family

- Have photographs of the child's birth family where she would most like to put them, e.g. in her bedroom, in a book, in the living room.

- Ensure that conversations about the birth family are carefully managed, so that the child does not have to make sense of negative, contradictory or idealised ideas about birth family members.

- Where direct or indirect contact is occurring, be actively involved in planning and facilitating contact so that the child's welfare is paramount and contact promotes security as well as roots and identity.

- Talk to the child's teacher about family issues that may unsettle the child, if raised in class.

Managing membership of more than one family

- Adults need to demonstrate their own flexibility about children's family memberships and what they might mean to the child.

- Both informally and in a planned way, talk with the child about the benefits and the challenges of having more than one family and help the child to understand and manage these relationships.

- Find models around the child of children who manage multiple families, e.g. in friends' families, on television, in books.

- Help the child to think about/talk about the inevitability of mixed feelings.

- Watch for possible pressure points, e.g. Mother's Day, Father's Day, Christmas, and find ways of indicating (where appropriate) that it is OK to give cards to more than one parent or to choose one rather than the other at different times.

- If necessary, talk to the child's teacher about family issues that may disturb the child if raised in class, i.e. help others outside the immediate family circle to be aware of the child's task in managing their multiple loyalties/families.

4 Using Secure Base: assessing prospective foster carers and adopters

This chapter provides guidance on the use of Secure Base when assessing prospective foster carers and adopters. The model provides a framework for considering the skills and capacities associated with offering therapeutic care as part of family life in foster care and adoption.

During the assessment, the five dimensions of the model will each be discussed in turn with prospective foster carers and adopters. These discussions can simply be part of routine information gathering. For example, when discussing the applicant's family background and close relationships, the question of how available they found their own parents may be a way to engage with the question of availability, and why it is important in building a child's trust and confidence.

The Secure Base dimensions can then be a framework for analysis and contribute to decision-making. Consideration will need to be given to applicants' skills and capacities within each dimension – as well as their capacity to develop those skills. Evidence of caregiving capacities can be sought in the previous and current life experiences of the applicants. This evidence need not necessarily be connected to parenting experience. For example, evidence of the capacity for co-operation might be found if an applicant has had to be appropriately assertive but also find a way of working together with others in their working life or community. Areas for further training and/or additional support can be highlighted. If there is very little evidence of the capacity to provide a secure base, this might contribute to the evidence to support a negative recommendation.

It will be helpful to use a laminated copy of the diagram of the Secure Base with applicants and to provide a brief description of the ideas behind the model (e.g. the links to promoting the child's development) to assist applicants in their understanding of the skills and capacities that they will need to evidence.

Availability – helping the child to trust

We know that the best environment for children's healthy emotional development is one in which they can take for granted that nurture, comfort and protection are readily available from caregivers when needed. This provides a secure base for exploration and allows children to begin to trust in themselves and others.

To provide a secure base, caregivers must be both *physically and emotionally available*. They must respond promptly, both when children and young people need closeness and protection and also when they are ready to move away and explore. They must have the capacity to reflect on what the child might be expecting from adults and then think flexibly about ways in which they can demonstrate to the child that they are reliable and trustworthy.

When assessing prospective caregivers it is important to help them to consider their capacity for physical and emotional availability as individuals, as a couple and as a family. This assessment must take into account the capacity to adapt to the different needs of individual children and the likelihood that children in care and adopted from care will find it difficult to trust.

AVAILABILITY: ISSUES FOR EXPLORATION IN ASSESSMENT

- The applicants' own experience of receiving/providing secure base availability, in childhood and adulthood, and the extent to which traumatic events and issues of loss and separation have been successfully resolved in the mind of the individual. When exploring this area, it is essential to move beyond general statements such as 'My mum was always there for me as a child' or 'I've always been there for my children' to examples and descriptive accounts of what happened/what that was like for them. For example, 'When I broke my arm and went to hospital, my mum didn't leave my side for a minute and I remember feeling really safe'.

- The extent to which applicants can demonstrate capacities for openness, availability and trust within their existing close relationships.

- The amount of physical time/emotional availability that the applicants have freely available to focus on the child's needs – this includes time to think and plan, time to respond to the child freely at key moments of the nurturing routine, e.g. mealtimes, bedtimes, before and after school, etc. But this also includes emotional space/energy to be an actively available and responsive caregiver.

- The balance of this availability for the child against time/emotional commitments to other family members, work, partnerships, interests, etc.

- Financial implications of this degree of availability and implications for financial support.

- The potential time/emotional needs of other family members, including the caregiver's own parents, five, 10, 15 years into the future.

- The caregiver's own career and life hopes and plans.

- The understanding of the long-term impact of early harm, the lengthy timescales involved in recovery and the likelihood of setbacks at crucial developmental stages (e.g. move to secondary school, exams, leaving school, moving towards independence, etc).

Sensitivity – helping the child to manage feelings

The capacity to tune in to the child, to be interested in what is in the child's mind, and to *see the world from the child's point of view* is key to helping children to manage difficult feelings and so be able to manage their behaviour. Caregivers must try to understand and make sense of what the child is thinking and feeling. They need to form flexible theories about this, so that they can respond sensitively and use a variety of techniques to help the child to make sense of himself. Caregivers must also support the child in experiencing and expressing the full range of emotions, and help him to manage and regulate them so they do not become overwhelming.

Additionally, caring for a troubled child can elicit a range of strong and often mixed feelings in the caregiver and it is important that these are acknowledged and discussed. Strong feelings in the caregiver may link to past or current relationships, but if feelings are overwhelming they can disable the caregiver just as they may disable the child.

SENSITIVITY: ISSUES FOR EXPLORATION IN ASSESSMENT

- The capacity to stand in the shoes of others/to think about what others might be thinking and feeling and be interested in the meanings behind behaviour.

- The capacity to think about and reflect on a range of feelings in self and others.

- The capacity to manage their own feelings and behaviours – and to see the connections between them.

- The capacity of all family members to show feelings appropriately and manage them in the best interests of the family.

- The capacity to think about and reflect on the range and mixture of feelings that a child might experience. These might include loss, dislocation, shock, fear, relief, excitement, disappointment, pleasure and so on.

- The capacity to think about and reflect on the reasons for certain feelings emerging and the links between feelings and behaviour in the child.

- The capacity to connect with their own feelings and behaviour at different life stages, especially adolescence.

- The capacity to tune into/stand in the shoes of young people who have experienced separations, loss and maltreatment in their early lives and to accept that the implications of difficult early experiences may be lifelong.

Acceptance – building the child's self-esteem

In order to restore or develop their self-esteem, children need caregivers who can accept them for who they are, for both their *strengths and their difficulties* and regardless of their differences or personalities. This level of acceptance will enable caregivers to identify and support their child's talents and interests, helping the child to fulfil his potential and feel good about himself.

If caregivers are to build self-esteem in this way, they must first be able to accept themselves, to feel comfortable with the people they are and to reflect this model of self-acceptance back to the child.

Families who have an ethos that 'nobody is good at everything but everybody is good at something' are well placed to identify and promote even the most deeply buried or unexpected abilities of their fostered or adopted children. At the same time, they can model that it is OK not to win, or not to be successful at everything.

ACCEPTANCE: ISSUES FOR EXPLORATION IN ASSESSMENT

- Indicators of positive self-esteem (acknowledgment of strengths and difficulties) in the applicants.

- The capacity to reflect on times of low self-esteem, recall feelings and behaviour, what helped or hindered recovery.

- Acceptance, enjoyment and capacity to embrace differences in culture, class, religion, ethnicity, etc.

- The capacity to identify and the commitment to support talents and interests.

- The capacity to understand that low self-esteem might be "masked" by boasting, unwillingness to take part in things, grandiosity, etc.

- The capacity to actively work on demonstrating acceptance/building self-esteem.

- The capacity to convey messages of acceptance that are comfortable and acceptable to children of different ages and with different needs.

- The capacity to connect with the issues that affect self-esteem in teenagers – identity, future pathways, peer pressure, etc.

- The capacity to be creative in providing opportunities for building self-esteem that are comfortable and acceptable to a range of different young people.

- The capacity to sustain their own self-esteem when under stress, and sustain/adapt their own interests and activities over time.

Co-operation – helping the child to feel effective

In order to help children to feel effective and competent, caregivers must think in terms of *working together* and forming a *co-operative alliance*. Children and young people may present as too powerful and controlling or as powerless and unable to assert themselves.

In all cases, caregiving will involve setting firm boundaries, but being prepared to negotiate within them and actively creating situations in which children and young people can make positive choices and decisions and be appropriately assertive.

Caregivers, therefore, must be able to enjoy co-operation and have at their disposal a range of approaches to achieve compromise. This will lead them to structure the child's environment so that there are plenty of safe opportunities for choice and autonomy.

To achieve a co-operative approach, caregivers will need a good understanding of themselves and the extent to which they need to be in control or find it hard to take control. The capacity for self-reflection is, therefore, also important in this area.

CO-OPERATION: ISSUES FOR EXPLORATION IN ASSESSMENT

- The applicant's own early experiences of feeling effective and competent (and ability to provide convincing examples).

- The applicant's own experience of how control and co-operation were negotiated in their family of origin.

- Evidence of co-operative relationships or working towards compromise in the applicant's current life – within partnerships, wider family or community.

- The applicant's capacity to be collaborative and co-operative within the assessment process itself.

- The capacity to recognise the child's need to feel effective and competent, and to work towards promoting this, even in very small ways.

- The capacity to accept that a young person might need to experience age-appropriate independence, while at the same time having their younger child's needs met.

- The capacity to provide additional support to help young people to be appropriately assertive in relationships and situations outside the home.

- The capacity to accept developing autonomy and that young people may make inadvisable choices.

- At times of conflict, the capacity to provide clear and honest feedback to the young person, both about the consequences of their actions and the position of the carers.

- The capacity to stay with a young person who appears rejecting and hostile and to hold in mind the longer-term significance of themselves as a secure base for that young person in the future. Providing messages of hope, concern and interest at these times requires carers with particular resilience and "stickability".

- The capacity to think about the potential impact on all family members if issues of co-operation become difficult later on.

Family membership – helping the child to belong

A sense of family membership begins from birth and is important for healthy development. All adopted and fostered children are connected to more than one family and will need to benefit from the practical and emotional support of their adoptive or foster family, but also have a comfortable and realistic sense of both the strengths and the limitations of their birth family network.

In all cases, caregiving families must have the capacity both to absorb new members, often children whose backgrounds and experiences are very different from their own, and to be thoughtful, reflective and open towards the child and the birth family.

FAMILY MEMBERSHIP: ISSUES FOR EXPLORATION IN ASSESSMENT

- The capacity of the applicants' family to admit new members, but also to be flexible enough to allow those members to pass to and fro (physically and emotionally) across the family boundary as needed. Examples may be found of including non-family or extended family members in the past.

- The extent to which the family system communicates openly with other systems – schools, community groups, special interest groups, friends and neighbours.

- The attitudes of the family to the world outside the family boundary – is it regarded as safe and trustworthy or threatening and hostile?

- Tolerance of difference in beliefs, values, expectations. The extent to which family membership can be offered even if norms and values are different to those of the child.

- The readiness of all family members to be flexible in order to accommodate children coming into the family.

- The capacity to accept that the child may not be ready or able to commit themselves emotionally to a new family for a considerable time.

- The capacity to offer sensitive messages of family membership while at the same time, understanding and respecting the child's sense of connection to the birth family.

- The capacity to continue to offer unconditional family membership to children and young people who may not have similar interests, personalities and abilities.

- The capacity to accept that the child's question 'Which family do I really belong to?' can emerge and re-emerge over time and will need to be discussed sensitively each time.

- The understanding that many fostered and adopted young people have intense and complex feelings of responsibility, anger, idealism, longing or guilt regarding their birth families.

- The capacity to support a young person to explore birth family history, as a part of the process of making sense of the past.

5 Using Secure Base: assessing the capacity of caregivers to provide a secure base for children in their care

The Secure Base model may be used alongside other assessment frameworks to assess the capacities of caregivers to provide a secure base for a particular child. The Secure Base Interview is the key resource to help with the focus on the five dimensions – both the caregiving and the developmental goals – and uses the caregiving cycle to structure the questions. This section provides guidance on the use of the Secure Base Interview and the interview itself – the next section provides guidance on the analysis of the interview.

It is important to engage the foster carer or adoptive parent in using Secure Base, both when undertaking the interview and when using the model to plan approaches for helping the caregiver to help the child. This should be a collaborative process, whereby the caregiver is invited to reflect on information and ideas that emerge, and then engage in thinking about and generating caregiving approaches that might be successful.

An outline schedule for the interview is provided, but this should be adjusted to use language that is clear and understandable to the individual caregiver and appropriate to the placement. It is expected that the interview would be done in ONE session – so that all the dimensions are covered. This means moving through the dimensions in an organised and concise way, as the interview schedule suggests. During the interview, the focus is on gathering information; discussions about ideas for trying different caregiving approaches can happen after the whole interview is complete.

The interview can be used in a range of contexts and serve a variety of purposes. For example:

- At an early stage of a fostering or adoption placement, the interview can be used to help foster carers and adopters to tune in to the child's needs. It can identify areas for further development and support for the carer and the child.

- As part of the routine supervision of foster carers or support for adopters, the interview can help to set and monitor goals for the child's development and to develop the caregivers' capacities.

- As part of the foster carer's annual review, the interview can highlight caregiving capacities and identify areas for further development and support.

- When foster or adoptive placements are in difficulties, the interview can highlight the needs and strengths of the child or young person and the capacities of the caregivers. It can identify areas for further development and support.

- When children and young people are thought to be in need of more effective caregiving or to be at risk, the interview can highlight the safety, needs and strengths of the child or young person and the capacities of the caregivers. It can identify areas for further development and support in this placement, or action to safeguard the child or promote their well-being.

The Secure Base Interview provides a means of exploring with the current caregiver their approaches to the child's needs and behaviour within the five dimensions of caregiving. This approach places the relationship between the child and the caregiver at the centre of the discussion, but all areas of the child's life may be relevant, e.g. progress at school and how the caregiver supports this will affect self-esteem.

Within each dimension of the Secure Base model, the caregiver is asked for a *specific* example of an incident which illustrates the child's behaviour and their caregiving response. Generalised responses such as 'He always gets upset' or 'I always try to be helpful' are not adequate for this type of assessment.

The caregiver is then asked to think about what the child may have been thinking and feeling during this incident and why the behaviour might have occurred. This is followed by a discussion about how the caregiver thought and felt about the child's behaviour at the time and how they responded. The incident can then be put in the context of ongoing issues regarding, for example, the child's ability to trust.

The Secure Base Interview

The following questions are about how (child's name) is developing and also about how you care for him or her. The discussion will help us to see what is going well and to think about any additional support that might be helpful to you and the child. I will ask you some questions about a time when the child behaved in a particular way – and then about how you responded and how that went, so that we can explore a range of different situations.

NB The diagram of the Secure Base model would be shown at the start with an explanation that the discussion will follow the five points of the star.

SECTION 1   **A brief description of the child/young person**

- Could you give me a brief description of (child)? Just the first things that come into your mind when you think of him/her.

  The caregiver should be asked to describe just the first things that come to mind about the child. Encourage a brief response to avoid straying into other areas of the interview. This introductory question is intended to "surprise the unconscious", as it asks for a spontaneous response that captures something of their ideas and feelings about the child.

SECTION 2   **Availability – helping the child to trust**

The following set of questions is about how far (the child) is able to trust in close adults. We will be thinking about what happens when he/she is upset or worried about something.

- Can you think of a particular time when he/she was upset or worried about something?

- What did (child) do?

- Why do you think he/she behaved in this particular way?

- What do you think he/she was thinking and feeling?

- What did you do at this time?

- How did that work out?

- How did (the child's) behaviour make you feel?

- Does the child usually behave in this way when upset?

- Was this your usual approach when he/she behaves in this way?

- Have you found other ways of helping?

SECTION 3   **Sensitivity – helping the child to manage feelings**

The following set of questions is about how far (the child) is able to manage his/her feelings. Children vary a great deal in how they manage strong feelings such as anger: some children show them easily, some go "over the top", some bottle them up.

- Can you think of a particular time when he/she was angry about something?

- What did (child) do when he/she felt angry?

- Why do you think he/she behaved in this particular way?

- What do you think he/she was thinking and feeling?

- What did you do at this time?

- How did that work out?
- How did (the child's) behaviour make you feel?
- Does the child usually behave in this way when he/she has strong feelings?
- Was this your usual approach when he/she behaves in this way?
- Have you found other ways of helping?

SECTION 4   Acceptance – building the child's self-esteem

The following set of questions is about how (child) feels about him/herself and how he/she copes if things don't go well.

Part 1

- Can you think of a particular time when (child) showed that they felt good about him/herself? *(NB If there are no examples, go to Part 2).*
- What did (child) do when he/she had these feelings?
- Why do you think he/she behaved in this particular way?
- What do you think he/she was thinking and feeling?
- What did you do at this time?
- How did that work out?
- How did (the child's) behaviour make you feel?
- Does the child usually behave in this way when he/she feels good about him/herself?
- Was this your usual approach when he/she behaves in this way?

Part 2

- Can you think of a particular time when things did not go well for (child) (for example, he/she was disappointed about something, lost a game, was not successful at something)?
- What did (child) do when this happened?
- Why do you think he/she behaved in this particular way?
- What do you think he/she was thinking and feeling?
- What did you do at this time?
- How did this work out?
- How did (the child's) behaviour at this time make you feel?
- Does the child usually behave in this way when things don't go well?
- Was this your usual approach when he/she shows low self-esteem?

- Have you found other ways of helping?

SECTION 5 **Co-operation – helping the child to feel effective**

The following questions are about how effective and competent (child) feels.

- How does (child) usually manage when given a task they find challenging?
- Can you give a particular example? How did he/she behave?
- Why do you think he/she behaved in this particular way?
- What do you think he/she was thinking and feeling?
- What did you say and/or do at this time?
- How did this work out?
- How did (the child's) behaviour at this time make you feel?
- Was this your usual approach when the child has a task to do?
- Have you found other ways of helping?

SECTION 6 **Family membership – helping the child to belong**

The following questions are about how (child) feels about belonging to this family.

- Can you think of a particular time when (child) has said or done something that shows how he/she feels about being part of your family?
- What did (child) say and/or do?
- Why do you think he/she spoke or behaved in this particular way?
- What do you think he/she was thinking and feeling?
- What did you say and/or do?
- How did this work out?
- How did (the child's) behaviour/what (the child) said at this time make you feel?
- Was this your usual approach?
- Have you found other ways of responding?

The following questions are about (child's) feelings about his/her birth family.

- Can you think of a particular time when (child) has said or done something that shows how he/she feels about his/her birth family?
- What did (child) say and/or do?
- Why do you think he/she spoke or behaved in this particular way?

- What do you think he/she was thinking and feeling?

- What did you say and/or do at this time?

- How did this work out?

- Was this your usual approach when (the child) shows his/her feelings about/ wants to talk about his/her birth family?

- How did (the child's) behaviour/what (the child) said at this time make you feel?

- Have you found other ways of responding?

Section 7   **Caregiving and support**

- What aspects of caring for this child give you the greatest *sense of pride or achievement*?

- What has been or is *the most difficult*?

- What are the major sources of help and support for you as a caregiver for this child?

- Can you think of any particular help that you would like with any of the things that we have discussed or any other aspect of caring for this child?

Analysis of the Secure Base Interview

SECTION 1   A brief description of the child/young person

Strengths in the relationship might be indicated by:

- Caregiver able to provide a description that includes concise evidence and is specific to this child.

- Caregiver shows warmth, interest, pleasure in the child.

- Description is balanced in terms of strengths and difficulties of the child and their feelings about him/her.

Difficulties in the relationship might be indicated by:

- Caregiver can provide only vague, generalised information (for example, "just an ordinary little girl").

- Caregiver is "cool", detached and appears to lack interest in the child. Or indicates hostility, sees child as a burden, or appears frightened of the child.

- Description of child is largely negative and critical.

SECTION 2   Availability – helping the child to trust

The child's capacity to trust is developed in the context of a caregiver who is physically and emotionally available. The Secure Base Interview addresses the issue of trust by focusing on the child's capacity to seek comfort when anxious or upset, i.e. to trust that a close adult will be available and responsive at these times, and then return to play and exploration.

For this section of the assessment, it can be helpful to consider secure and insecure attachment patterns to help make sense of how the child behaves when he or she is stressed. This is not about classifying the child, but more about looking for patterns in behaviour and understanding the child's coping strategies. It is also important to establish how the caregiver may be responding to the child's coping strategies (e.g. when a child shuts down on their feelings) and whether their response is supporting greater security, as a secure base should, or reinforcing insecurity.

Securely attached children

A secure child will have the capacity to use the caregiver as a secure base, providing comfort, reassurance and support when the child encounters difficulties and enabling the child to return to play and exploration. For example, a toddler might play happily, away from the caregiver, but glance back or vocalise to the caregiver to ensure that they are still there. However, if the child hurts himself, he will run immediately to the caregiver for comfort. The quality of the exploration – relaxed, inquisitive, absorbed – is important here. Comfort-seeking for a secure child is a means to an end – the end being to reduce anxiety and to restore equilibrium so that further exploration and activity can occur.

Insecurely attached children

Children with **avoidant** attachment patterns are less able to use the caregiver as a secure base and may try to be self-reliant when in difficulty. The child is not avoiding a relationship with the caregiver, but rather is avoiding displays of emotion, especially negative emotion, in order not to cause stress to the caregiver and to maintain some kind of physical closeness. The child may seem well-behaved, focus on toys or activities rather than seek comfort and may appear "unmoved" by difficult events. Such children may mistakenly be seen as "resilient" or said to have no attachment, when in fact they are highly anxious but their learned strategy is to minimise attachment behaviours because they lack trust in the response.

Children who have **ambivalent** attachment patterns have learned to get their needs met by showing their emotions and making constant demands in the hope of achieving the caregiver's availability and attention. These children may retreat to the caregiver when they are upset, indeed they may be clinging to the caregiver much of the time, but without being able to explore, play and learn. Children cannot move confidently away from the caregiver because they do not trust that the caregiver will continue to be there for them if they do so. This may lead to very demanding behaviour, with switches between extremes of neediness and anger. But it can lead to helpless and hopeless behaviour, with neediness being the dominant emotion.

Children with **disorganised** attachment patterns, who have experienced frightened or frightening parenting, are left with a dilemma – how do I approach someone for comfort when they will raise my anxiety rather than reduce it? Infants and very young children are left without any effective strategy and they may display confused and confusing behaviour – perhaps "freezing" in the presence of the caregiver, or approaching and then turning away.

Beyond infancy, children with disorganised attachment patterns start to use a range of behavioural strategies that are designed to control the carer and make the environment more predictable. These behaviours (punitive aggression, compulsive self-reliance, compulsive caregiving) can already be developing in the pre-school years and make it difficult to interpret what the child is thinking and feeling.

When the child with a disorganised attachment pattern is not so stressed that they show these more extreme behaviours, their behaviour is likely to be consistent with either avoidant or ambivalent patterns/strategies.

Caregiver's strengths in availability/helping the child to trust

- Plenty of physical time available to focus on the child.

- Emotional space and availability (i.e. not preoccupied with own difficult feelings and unmet needs or emotionally detached and cut off).

- The capacity to reflect on the child's needs to build trust in them as caregiver(s) and to think about ways in which they might support the child to do so.

- Being alert to the child's needs and signals (e.g. able to identify and describe a time when the child was worried or upset, how the child showed this/did not show it, what signs they might look for in the child to signal distress, etc).

Caregiver's difficulties in availability/helping the child to trust

- Lack of time/energy.

- The caregiver's unmet needs (perhaps from the past) are coming to the fore.

- The caregiver seems overwhelmed by the child's demands.

- The caregiver feels marginalised by the child.

- The caregiver distances themselves from the child.

- The caregiver doesn't believe a child should need that much attention.

SECTION 3   Sensitivity – helping the child to manage feelings

Critical to children's ability to engage comfortably and constructively with play or school work, as well as in their relationships with family and friends, is their ability to manage or regulate their feelings and behaviour. Being overwhelmed by feelings such as *anxiety* or *anger* makes it very difficult for children to become competent and confident in play, learning or activities with others.

The Secure Base Interview focuses on how the child manages difficult feelings, such as anger or distress, as this is often one of the most problematic areas for troubled children of all ages. However, it may also be helpful to gather information about if and how the child expresses *a range* of feelings, such as sadness or happiness: are they being appropriately expressed, or suppressed or expressed explosively and excessively? Verbal and non-verbal, direct and indirect communication of feelings will be relevant. For instance, the interview (and the broader assessment from health and education sources) may include reports of rages and tantrums, but also headaches, tummy aches, bed-wetting, or self-harm at times of stress for the child.

The social worker should be aware that the child's capacity to express and manage the full range of feelings appropriately in relationships relies on mind-mindedness or the capacity to mentalise (i.e. the child's ability to think about what they and what other people might be thinking and feeling) and make links to behaviour. In infancy it is the mind-mindedness of the caregiver which contains and regulates the child's feelings. But as the growing child spends increasing amounts of time away from the caregiver, they will need to think about their own mind and the minds of others in order to regulate their own feelings and behaviour and take account of the feelings of others, showing empathy for example. This developmental shift in healthy emotional and cognitive development occurs when a child is around 3–4 years old. For children from backgrounds of abuse and neglect, this capacity is likely to be impaired and will only develop in the context of a new secure base relationship.

Of concern is the need to identify and understand patterns of behaviour that would indicate the coping or defensive strategies adopted by a child when strong feelings surface, or the lack of strategy and dysregulation that leads to extreme aggressive behaviours or to denial and dissociation. Important then, is how the caregiver responds.

Caregiver's strengths in sensitivity/helping the child to manage feelings

- The caregiver can think and talk about the child's feelings and how they are expressed, recognise that the child has strong feelings at times, and that they are understandable, in the circumstances.

- The caregiver has the capacity to "stand in the shoes" of the child, to think flexibly about what the child may be thinking and feeling and to reflect this back appropriately to the child.

- The caregiver can think and talk about their own feelings and share them appropriately with the child and other people.

Caregiver's difficulties in sensitivity/helping the child to manage feelings

- The caregiver lacks interest and curiosity in what is in the child's mind.

- The caregiver has difficulty in thinking flexibly about a range of possible feelings/reasons for the child behaving in a certain way.

- The caregiver finds it hard to think and talk about the child's past – finds it too painful or feels that the child needs a "fresh start".

- The caregiver is frequently negative or angry towards the child without a "pause for thought" about why the child is behaving in this way or how best to respond.

- The caregiver appears overwhelmed by their own strong feelings or finds it hard to think and talk about their own feelings. (NB There is a normal variation in talking about feelings; it is extremes that are of concern. Key is the capacity to acknowledge and understand the child's thoughts and feelings.)

SECTION 4   Acceptance – building the child's self-esteem

Children with good self-esteem are able to enjoy their success, take the risk of trying new things and accept that they cannot be good at everything. Healthy self-esteem, therefore, is often about aspiring to do well, while acknowledging realistically what can and cannot be achieved.

Many children have difficulty in accepting and valuing themselves and the exact nature of this difficulty for each child needs careful attention within an assessment. The obvious starting point is the child's history, to see where there may have been some opportunities for the child to feel loved and valued or where particularly harsh forms of rejection or scapegoating may have occurred. The Secure Base Interview builds on this information by seeking specific examples of good self-esteem, poor self-esteem and the child's management of failure or setbacks.

Because children with low self-esteem have to *defend* against the feelings that this induces, what the child says openly is not likely to give you a straightforward or accurate picture. Smiles, boastfulness or an inability to accept failure, such as the loss of a game, may be masking very low self-esteem.

Accepting the self is not just about valuing personal qualities or perceived success, but is linked to a *developing self-concept and identity*. In this broader context, children's ability to accept and value their gender, ethnicity, community, culture and religion are important parts of the self-concept. In the minds of children who experience various degrees of disruption and discontinuity, being lovable or unlovable, a good or a bad person may become linked to being a girl, being of a particular ethnicity or having a disability.

Multiple sources of information and observation relating to self-esteem are important in assessment, planning and supporting placements, and in deciding whether to confirm a pattern or provide a window onto different aspects of the child's sense of self that need to be addressed.

Caregiver's strengths in acceptance/building the child's self-esteem

- The caregiver shows joy, pride and pleasure in the child and provides vivid examples.

- The caregiver can praise the child easily and readily.

- The caregiver can help the child to accept failures, setbacks, etc, in a kind, supportive way.

- The caregiver can actively support the child in pursuing (child-led) experiences, interests and activities.

Caregiver's difficulties in acceptance/building the child's self-esteem

- A tendency to focus on negative aspects of the child, with little evident pleasure or pride.

- Finding it hard to accept/enjoy the child's individuality and ways in which the child may be different to other family members.

- The caregiver sees the child as a "burden".

- The caregiver offers little active support to the child in pursuing (child-focused) experiences, interests and activities.

SECTION 5   Co-operation – helping the child to feel effective

The more *appropriately* effective and assertive a child is able to be, the more likely it is that the child will co-operate and compromise. Such a child has learned that assertiveness *combined* with willingness to make some concessions and co-operate with others is most likely to achieve their goals *and* maintain valued relationships.

The Secure Base Interview includes a focus both on the child's capacity to feel effective and competent and the extent to which the child can therefore both assert him/herself and co-operate/work together with adults.

The assessment of effectiveness is rarely straightforward and this area may need additional consideration and analysis. Some children's sense of effectiveness has been so undermined that they cannot assert themselves at all and they behave in a dependent and passive way. Other children become so frightened by their own powerlessness that they can only feel comfortable when they are in total control of others – and so *seem* very powerful. Similarly, being undemanding and self-reliant can actually be quite controlling, since the message to the parent is 'I won't let you look after me'. Even very dependent children can be controlling, with the message 'I won't let you get on with your life – I need you too much.'

Because of the nature and complex links between *effectiveness* and *co-operation*, the assessment needs to look at them separately and together.

Caregiver's strengths in co-operation/helping the child to feel effective

- The caregiver thinks about the child as an autonomous individual whose wishes, feelings and goals are valid and meaningful and who needs to feel effective (for example, 'He gets settled with his toys and it's understandable that he hates it when we have to go out').

- The caregiver can look for ways of working together to achieve enjoyable co-operation with the child wherever possible (for example, 'We make a game of clearing the toys up and he enjoys that so he doesn't mind going out so much').

- The caregiver promotes choice and effectiveness wherever possible.

- The caregiver can set safe and clear boundaries and limits – and also negotiate within them.

Caregiver's difficulties in co-operation/helping the child to feel effective

- The caregiver emphasises the need for control, for example, differences of opinion with the child are a battle that they must win.

- The caregiver finds it difficult to accept/enjoy the child's need for autonomy and to allow choice/promote competence and effectiveness.

- The caregiver finds it difficult to allow the child to try new things or take moderate risks.

SECTION 6   Family membership – helping the child to belong

Family membership is a vital strand of emotional and psychosocial development. Assessment of this dimension requires a great deal of sensitivity to the child's experiences and views, but also to the very different ways in which families work and family membership is expressed. There are also important links to the child's need to develop a coherent sense of identity through making sense of connections to more than one family.

For children who are separated from their birth families, the nature of birth family and foster or adoptive family membership will vary according to the type of placement, the child's stage of development, and the quality and meaning of family relationships to the child. This section of the assessment will therefore need to be adjusted accordingly.

If the family placement arrangements are planned to be permanent, consideration will have to be given to the extent to which they offer support for the child to become a happy, settled, secure, resilient and pro-social member of the family and the community into adulthood.

All families define their boundaries differently and develop very varied ways of signalling to each other and the outside world that 'We belong together'. They also vary in the extent to which they include this particular child within their family boundary. Differences may be based on culture, class or ethnicity or simply ways of talking about "family". These differences need to be listened to with care.

However, differences in messages of membership of the foster or adoptive family may also be about this child and whether this child is willing or able to fit in with the family's expectations of its members. Therefore, the way in which the child talks, is talked to and is talked about in the family will vary in meaning but will always be significant. The meanings and long-term value of family relationships and memberships for the particular child cannot be judged on simple criteria, such as whether or not foster carers are called "Mum and Dad", when children's connections to multiple families are so much more complex than that.

Caregiver's strengths in family membership/helping the child to belong

- The caregiver is able to give verbal and non-verbal messages of the child's inclusion in the family.

- The caregiver is able to talk openly and appropriately with the child about both the strengths and the difficulties of their birth family.

- The caregiver is able to support the child sensitively in managing their thoughts/feelings about their foster or adoptive family and their birth family and in presenting their situation to the outside world.

- The caregiver can support the child with contact appropriate to their needs and the care plan.

Caregiver's difficulties in family membership/helping the child to belong

- The caregiver tends to treat the child differently/less considerately to other children in the family (for example, providing different sort of food for a lunchbox).

- The caregiver talks/thinks negatively about the birth family and fails to understand the child's need to have some positive sense of their birth family connections.

- The caregiver creates (unreasonable) barriers to connections/contact between the child and the birth family.

SECTION 7   Caregiving and support

The final section of the interview sums up the caregiver's feelings about the child and explores, with the caregiver, the range and type of support available and the caregiver's willingness to seek and use support.

Caregiver's strengths in caregiving and support

- The caregiver showing pleasure/satisfaction in their caregiving role for this child and being willing to/having accepted support.

- The caregiver being able to identify difficulties, but not be overwhelmed by them.

- The caregiver being open to the idea that they may need additional advice and knowledge.

- The caregiver indicating that they have tried and tested strategies and people that they can rely on for practical and emotional support.

Caregiver's difficulties in caregiving and support

- The caregiver lacking pleasure and pride in caring for the child and being unwilling to consider outside help and advice to achieve change.

- The caregiver denying difficulties or appearing overwhelmed by them.

- The caregiver being pessimistic/fatalistic about the child's capacity to change or their capacity to contribute to that change.

- The caregiver lacking support or denying the need for support.

Additional resources

The Secure Base Checklist (Chapter 7) provides detailed questions to support the analysis/assessment of children's emotional and relationship development at different chronological ages and stages and across the five dimensions.

6 Using Secure Base: supporting caregivers

Secure Base can be used to support the full range of foster carers and adoptive parents and is relevant for the care of children and young people of all ages. It can be used:

- in planning a support package to accompany a match between a child and a new family;

- at the beginning of a fostering or adoption placement;

- as part of the regular supervision/support of foster carers or the support service provided to adoptive parents;

- when fostering or adoptive placements are in difficulties;

- when children and young people are thought to be in need of more effective caregiving or at risk.

The most productive way of getting started where a child is in placement is for the Secure Base Interview to be carried out first. This will assess the strengths and difficulties of the child and the caregiver and provide indicators for further development and support. At the end of the interview, it would be expected that the worker and the caregiver would discuss together some of the conclusions they may reach about what is going well and what is not going so well in the placement and in the relationship between the caregiver and the child. This will then inform the use of the model and each dimension.

The Secure Base star diagram (Figure 2, p. 16) should be used in all work with caregivers and a laminated copy should be left with the caregiver between sessions. Copies of each dimension cycle could also be left with the caregivers as they get discussed. The Secure Base Progress Record (see Resources) can be used to record and review each session.

Introducing the caregiving cycle

- Emphasise that the approach that you will be taking is strengths-based. It will highlight the positive caregiving that is already occurring in the family and build on this.

- Show a diagram of the **caregiving cycle**.

- Explain the **caregiving cycle**. Explain that thinking and feeling always affect behaviour, both in children and adults. This will be explored further in the sessions.

- Discuss examples from the caregiver's day-to-day experience with the child in their care in order to explore the link between thoughts, feelings and behaviour in caregivers and in children.

Exploring each Secure Base dimension with caregivers

- Explain the dimension to the caregiver – the idea/theory behind each dimension and why it is important to children's development.

- Explore the child's needs in relation to the dimension.

- Explore and develop the caregiver's thinking and feeling in relation to the dimension.

- Promote the caregiver's sense of competence in the dimension by highlighting existing positive caregiving approaches and building on them, or developing new ones. (Have some practical suggestions for the caregiver to try – appeal to their creativity.)

- Help the caregiver to look for and value even small signs of progress in the child in relation to the dimension.

- Promote the caregiver's awareness of the links between all five dimensions.

Availability – helping the child to trust

Explaining this dimension to the caregiver

- Explore the concept of trust in availability of a secure base, i.e. when children can trust that an adult will always be there to support them (a safe haven), they are free to play, explore and develop. When children do not trust in the availability of an adult, they are anxious, cannot play, concentrate, learn and develop. Anxiety shows itself in "difficult" behaviour – from infancy to adolescence.

- Help the caregiver to understand this concept by asking them to think about experiences in their own lives when they were anxious and had someone to turn to – what did this allow them to do?

- And at times when they had no one to turn to – what was the effect of this?

Exploring the child's needs

- How far can the child trust in you? In others? In him or herself? Discuss examples from the child's everyday life.

Exploring and developing the caregiver's thinking and feeling

- Explore personal issues if relevant. Help the caregiver to recognise how their own early experiences of availability might help and, sometimes, hinder them as caregivers for this child. Advise further help if severe difficulties are emerging.

- Discuss what is known about the experiences of this child during the infancy/pre-school years. Discuss what impact (positive and negative) these experiences might have had on their ability to trust in themselves and other people.

- Help the caregiver to understand that they are often meeting children's unmet needs from a much earlier period. These needs will diminish as trust develops.

Promoting availability

- Discuss the child's needs and signals. How does this child signal a need for closeness? And a need to explore? How can the caregiver make time and availability to respond? If the child's signals are weak or absent, how can the caregiver structure them for the child (e.g. the child does not cry when hurt. The caregiver might offer sympathetic words and gestures, talk about how the hurt might feel, offer acceptable closeness – a hug, a story, etc).

- Consider new **caregiving approaches that promote trust** (see above p. 19). Discuss how to adapt these to suit the age and needs of the child and/or develop others that are likely to be comfortable/effective for the caregiver and the child.

- Acknowledge possible difficulties, show empathy and acceptance and offer support for change.

Helping the caregiver to find and value signs of progress in the child

- Discuss and record signs (however small) of the child's increased capacity to trust, increased competence and confidence.

- Discuss and record any indicators (however small) that the child is thinking: 'I matter', 'I am safe', 'I can explore and return', 'Other people can be trusted'.

- Set goals/agree on approaches for the carer to try before the next session (may use the Secure Base Progress Record).

Promoting awareness of the links between all five dimensions

- Link to next dimension – using the Secure Base star diagram. Explain that trust and availability are necessary to help children to learn to manage their feelings.

Sensitivity – helping the child to manage feelings

Explaining this dimension to the caregiver

- Sensitivity, in this context, refers to the caregiver's capacity to "stand in the shoes" of the child, to think flexibly about what the child may be thinking and feeling and to reflect this back to the child. This helps the child to think about, make sense of, and manage their feelings and behaviour.

- The sensitive caregiver also thinks about their own feelings and shares them appropriately with the child.

- This helps the child to value her own ideas and feelings and the thoughts and feelings of others.

- Discuss how important it is for a child to know about feelings – to be able to name their own feelings AND to understand that having mixed feelings (for example, feelings of love and anger towards the same person) is normal and OK.

- Discuss how important it is for children to understand other people's thoughts and feelings. For example, a child who wants to join in a game needs to think about what other children might be thinking (Will he spoil our game? Will he play by the rules?) in order to successfully take part.

Exploring the child's needs

- Is this child able to express feelings appropriately?

- How far can this child manage their feelings, e.g. does she "overflow" with strong feelings – anger, sadness, excitement, etc.? Or are feelings repressed and denied?

- Can the child acknowledge mixed feelings?

- Can the child name feelings appropriately?

Exploring and developing the caregiver's thinking and feeling

- Helping the caregiver to tune in to the child – thinking about the mind of this child – use examples/incidents of being able to tune in to what the child is thinking and feeling.

- Discuss what is in the mind of the child when she is at her best. What is in the mind of the child when she is at her most difficult?

- Help the caregiver to reflect on their own thinking and feeling/increased self-awareness, e.g. how does the child make you feel as a parent? How do you show/manage those feelings?

- Help the caregiver to understand that it is important to discuss/share those feelings with a supportive person and sometimes to show/discuss them (appropriately) with the child. Discuss ways of doing this.

- Acknowledge their strengths as a caregiver in this dimension.

- Acknowledge their possible difficulties as a caregiver and show empathy, acceptance, and offer support for change.

Promoting sensitivity

- Discuss ways of helping the child to understand, express and manage feelings appropriately.

- Consider new **caregiving approaches that help manage feelings** (see above p. 22). Adapt these to suit the age and needs of the child and/or develop others that are likely to be comfortable for the child.

Helping the caregiver to find and value signs of progress in the child

- Discuss and record signs (however small) of increased capacity to manage feelings – to express feelings more appropriately.

- Discuss and record any indicators (however small) that the child is thinking: 'My feelings make sense', 'I can manage my strong feelings', 'Other people have thoughts and feelings that I need to take into account'.

- Set goals/agree on approaches to try before the next session (may use Secure Base Progress Record).

Promoting awareness of the links between all five dimensions

- Link back to availability – the carer needs to be emotionally and physically available and the child needs to experience trust in order to manage feelings.

- Link forward to acceptance – showing that the child's feelings are understood and accepted is part of acceptance and helps to build self-esteem. But self-esteem needs a special focus.

Acceptance – building the child's self-esteem

Explaining this dimension to the caregiver

- For all children, it is important to be unconditionally accepted and valued for who they are, for their difficulties as well as their strengths. This forms the foundation of positive self-esteem, so that children can feel worthy of receiving love, help and support and also be able to deal with setbacks and failures.

- Many children who have had a difficult start in life have very low self-esteem. This can be seen even in young babies.

Exploring the child's needs

- How does this child feel about herself?

- How does she cope with new experiences, activities, etc?

- How does she accept praise?

- How does she cope with failure and setbacks?

Exploring and developing the caregiver's thinking and feeling

- Help the caregiver to reflect on self-esteem in their own lives – what made them feel good about themselves in their childhood/how were they helped to cope with setbacks?

- Discuss how caregivers are looking after themselves at this time. Discuss practical ways of improving this if needed (for example, taking time out, spending time with friends, activities, etc). Explain that this is a positive model for the child AND will sustain their own confidence and self-esteem, especially if the child makes them feel like a "bad" parent.

- Acknowledge possible difficulties, show empathy and acceptance, and offer support for change.

Promoting acceptance

- Consider approaches already used to build self-esteem and manage setbacks. How might they be extended and developed?

- Consider new **caregiving approaches that build self-esteem** (see above p. 26). Adapt to suit the age and needs of the child and/or develop others that are likely to be comfortable for the child.

Helping the caregiver to find and value signs of progress in the child

- Discuss and record signs (however small) of improved self-esteem – taking more "risk" in unfamiliar situations, accepting a compliment, not having a tantrum when losing a game, etc.

- Discuss and record any indicators (however small) that the child is thinking: 'I am accepted and valued for who I am'.

- Set goals/agree on approaches for the carer to try before the next session (may use the Secure Base Progress Record).

Promoting the caregiver's awareness of the links between all five dimensions

- Crucially for caregivers, this area of parenting builds on the dimensions of *availability* and *sensitivity*. Children need to learn to trust and to manage their feelings and behaviour in order to believe the praise of carers and to take up opportunities that are on offer.

- Acceptance is also linked to co-operation/helping children to be effective.

Co-operation – helping the child to feel effective

Explaining this dimension to the caregiver

- Children need to be able to compromise and co-operate. Without co-operation, family, school and peer relationships become a battle – with winners and losers.

- Co-operation means shared but not equal power – caregivers must protect children and keep them safe and also have their own priorities.

- Children find it hard to co-operate if they feel powerless. Children are more likely to co-operate if they feel effective and competent.

Exploring the child's needs

- How effective does this child feel? Does she need to be "in control" or does she find it hard to assert herself appropriately?

- How does the child feel about making choices? Think about simple things such as what to wear, eat, etc.

Exploring and developing the caregiver's thinking and feeling

- Help caregivers to be aware of feelings of competence/effectiveness in their earlier lives – and lack of effectiveness.

- Discuss how this might have affected how they manage issues of power, control and compromise now – with adults and with children.

- Help caregivers to see that co-operation is not a sign of weakness or giving in to a child. Working together provides a positive model for the child. Setting clear limits but allowing for choice and compromise within them ensures the child's safety and keeps the adults appropriately in control.

- Acknowledge possible difficulties, show empathy and acceptance and offer support for change.

Promoting co-operation

- Consider approaches already used to promote the child's competence, effectiveness and capacity to co-operate. How might they be extended and developed?

- Consider new **caregiving approaches that promote competence and co-operation** (see p. 30). Adapt to suit the age and needs of the child and/or develop others that are likely to be comfortable for the child.

Helping the caregiver to find and value signs of progress in the child

- Discuss and record signs (however small) of improved effectiveness, competence and co-operation.

- Discuss and record any indicators (however small) that the child is thinking: 'I can make things happen within safe limits', 'I can compromise and co-operate'.

- Set goals/agree on approaches to try before next session (may use the Secure Base Progress Record).

Promoting the caregiver's awareness of the links between all five dimensions

- Make links between dimensions: availability, sensitivity and acceptance – all contribute to children's sense of self-value and capacity to negotiate and compromise, BUT children may need direct help to feel effective.

Family membership – helping the child to belong

Explaining this dimension to the caregiver

- Family membership is a vital strand of healthy emotional and psychosocial development. A child who has no close family relationships will feel psychologically and socially isolated. In contrast, the certainty of unconditional family membership provides anchorage and reassurance – enabling exploration and personal development.

- When children are separated from their birth families, this dimension refers to the capacity of the foster or adoptive caregiver to include the child, socially and personally as a full family member, in a way that is appropriate to the longer term plan for the child. At the same time, the caregiver must help the child to establish an appropriate sense of connectedness to his birth family.

  NB The different roles of foster or adoptive family membership and birth family membership/sense of connection vary according to the type of placement and the child's stage of development and this will need to be discussed accordingly.

Exploring the child's needs

- All children and young people, even those in short-term placements, value a sense of inclusion and of being treated as part of the foster/adoptive family.

- A positive sense of family membership can occur (and be beneficial to the child) in foster, adoptive or birth families even if the relationship is not emotionally close, i.e. it is about having a sense of loyalty and shared identity.

- Children need help to manage partial information about the past and also their mixed feelings about connections to their different families.

Exploring and developing the caregiver's thinking and feeling

- Discuss with caregivers their own sense of family membership. What are their experiences in their families of origin? How do they promote a sense of family membership in their current family? Do they have a strongly defined family identity or is it less clearly defined/more flexible?

- How do they feel in relation to offering family membership to this child?

- If the child is separated from the birth family, how do they feel about the child's current sense of birth family membership?

- Acknowledge possible difficulties and show empathy and acceptance.

Promoting family membership

- Think about the family membership needs of this child: 'How can we help this child get the best from both families?'

- Consider approaches already used to promote family membership or a sense of connection in both families. How might they be extended and developed?

- Consider new **caregiving approaches that build family membership** (see p. 33). Adapt to suit the age and needs of the child and/or develop others that are likely to be comfortable for the child.

Helping the caregiver to find and value signs of progress in the child

- Discuss and record signs (however small) of a comfortable sense of family membership/connection in either/both families.

- Discuss and record any indicators (however small) that the child is thinking: 'I can belong comfortably or feel connected to both of my families'.

- Set goals/agree on approaches to try before next session (may use the Secure Base Progress Record).

Promoting the caregiver's awareness of the links between all five dimensions

- Link to all dimensions – family membership can be promoted through availability, being sensitive to the feelings of this child, accepting this child for who she is, and working together co-operatively as a family.

7 Using Secure Base: assessing and reviewing the development of fostered and adopted children

Social workers and other professionals involved with the fostered or adopted child will need to undertake their own assessments of the child's development and functioning in order to ascertain the effectiveness of the caregiving and determine the progress the child is making. Although one significant outcome of a foster carer or adopter receiving support with secure base parenting is that they show increased capacity to offer caregiving across the five secure base dimensions, the goal is to see the developmental benefit in terms of outcomes for the child across the five dimensions.

Gathering relevant information and conducting an assessment of the child's development using the *Secure Base Checklist* (see below) may help by reassuring both the caregiving family and the professional network that the child is progressing well. It may also identify where there is a need for additional support for the child, the caregiver, the family or other agencies, on one or more dimension. For example, problems with contact or education may lead to additional support being provided to the child, the caregiver, the birth family or the school. In some cases, assessment on one or more dimensions may raise concerns about a child or placement that need to be addressed more urgently.

Actions or interventions that follow this assessment will depend on the degree of urgency or need. But in most cases, there will be a discussion with the caregiver about the child's progress and an invitation to determine jointly which area the caregiver will work on first. Although trust is an obvious starting point for many children, it may be that for some children, self-esteem or family membership are the first issues that need to be addressed. This discussion is likely to lead back to issues regarding trust, so that all five dimensions are included.

Framework for assessment

The dimensions can be used to provide a framework for the assessment of the child's developmental status and progress in a placement. Within each age group the *key developmental tasks* for this stage will be explored, matching them across the secure base dimensions. It is important to bear in mind the child's emotional as well as chronological age – so questions from a younger age group may well be relevant to older children.

To complete the checklist, there are questions about specific aspects of the child's behaviour that require evidence. Many of these questions will bring evidence from different sources – the caregiver's account; direct observation and work with the child; information from other key people, e.g. health visitor or teacher. However, for each question it should be possible for the caregiver or other informant to provide *evidence,* e.g. for trust, was there a specific occasion when the infant or child showed trust in a particular caregiver?

It is also possible that, following a detailed discussion, a rating scale for each dimension might be used, e.g. the child's capacity to trust might be rated on a scale of 0–10. This would provide a global picture that could be reviewed over time. For some dimensions it may be helpful to break down these scales, e.g. with family membership, it may be possible to rate how well the child is managing being part of the foster or adoptive family with a separate rating of how they are managing their relationship with the birth family.

There will be a different emphasis on different dimensions for children of different ages. For example, the family membership dimension is less significant in infancy but for older children is a key part of their identity. There are also appropriate variations in the child's sense of belonging to foster families depending on the placement and the care plan. But even in short-term placements all children, including infants and toddlers, need to feel that they are treated and valued as part of the family during their stay.

Secure Base Checklist

Infants 0 – 18 months

Key tasks for the infant in this period include the development of selective and secure attachment relationships and the use of these secure base relationships to develop pleasure in exploration, play and learning.

The questions below therefore focus on the infant's capacity to seek comfort from specific caregivers when in need or distress, their capacity to accept comfort and their capacity to experience pleasure in exploration when their anxiety is recognised, understood and soothed. So the child's signs of activity and pleasure in play and exploration are as important as comfort-seeking behaviours in assessing the quality of attachment relationships and the child's developmental progress.

This is a period of rapid change so attention needs to be paid to age appropriateness in each area, e.g. selectivity of attachment, competence in communicating emotions. Even from birth, infants are communicating their feelings in some form. But also from birth, there will be some differences in levels of sociability and activity due to differences in temperament. The normal range of developmental needs must be taken into account.

Trust

Does the child:

- seek comfort when distressed (e.g. crying and gazing towards the caregiver)?

- accept comfort when distressed (e.g. settling when picked up and cuddled)?

- show some degree of preference for one or more caregiver (e.g. gaze/preferred for cuddles – develops during the first 6–8 months)?

- target attachment behaviours at this caregiver/these caregivers (e.g. gaze, verbalisation when upset/happy – approach once mobile)?

- protest at separation from specific caregivers (NB range of protest behaviour – depending on temperament/attachment pattern)?

- settle/settle to play at reunion?

- use a caregiver as a secure base for exploration (observable cycle of comfort and reassurance/exploration)?

- show interest and pleasure in the environment (facial expression, sensory exploration)?

- enjoy playing jointly/independently with objects/toys?

- take turns with/"converse" with adults – initiating and responding to vocalising, facial movements (can start from hours after birth)?

Managing feelings

Does the child:

- show a full range of emotions, both positive and negative (e.g. smile, laugh, frown, rage, cry)?

- communicate their needs (e.g. for proximity, food, play)?

- react appropriately to sensory stimuli (e.g. show interest/react to light, sound, smell, touch, taste – but not panic or freeze)?

- wait for attention/manage emotions – with help (e.g. voice of caregiver indicating food is on the way)?

- sleep regularly and in a relaxed way (NB sleep patterns will vary)?

- seem comfortable in their body (e.g. able to relax and also enjoy being active)?

- cope with being told "no" (e.g. protest but not become overwhelmed)?

Self-esteem

Does the child:

- express pleasure at their achievements (e.g. shaking a rattle to make a noise, standing up on their own, building a tower)?

- show interest and enthusiasm for interactive games like peek-a-boo (e.g. showing pleasure at success)?

- approach new people/situations positively (balancing curiosity, caution and pleasurable anticipation)?

- cope with setbacks (e.g. when the rattle doesn't work, or the brick tower falls over)?

Feeling effective

Does the child:

- make choices (e.g. between foods, toys)?

- assert himself (e.g. getting attention, feeding at his own pace)?

- seem keen to try new things (NB some variation in enjoying novelty due to differences in temperament)?

- show focus and persistence in their play (e.g. sustained activity to complete task)?

- co-operate with nappy changes, feeding, going to sleep (i.e. relaxing and accepting events with the reassurance of caregivers)?

- play co-operatively (e.g. turn-taking/accepting support to hold the rattle, pressing the button to make a sound, can lead to co-operative play even in infancy)?

Sense of belonging

Does the child:

- recognise family members (e.g. extend their recognition to family members other than caregivers)?

- prefer certain family members and family friends (e.g. more likely to communicate with/accept cuddles from)?

- enjoy family occasions (e.g. seem to fit in as part of the family – if supported/ not overwhelmed)?

18 MONTHS - 4 YEARS

Autonomy and dependency issues are particularly important in this period. Children will increasingly need to manage separations and the availability or otherwise of their caregivers as they first become more competent walkers and talkers and then become more sophisticated and independent in their play and relationships.

For 3–4-year-olds, it is the capacity to understand that other people have feelings and goals that are different from their own that is a key turning point developmentally. The child's emerging ability at this age to mentalise, to name and reflect on their own feelings, to be empathic about the feelings of others and to be able to take those feelings into account will be shaping the child's engagement not only with adult caregivers but also with the world of peer relationships.

Children who are insecure following insensitive parenting will suffer from difficulties in making sense of the thoughts and feelings of others, because they have not experienced carers who have fully tuned into and helped them make sense of their feelings. For children who have experienced abuse and neglect, this lack of social or emotional intelligence may be accompanied by more deep-rooted fears that can lead to the formation of controlling strategies at this age.

The assessment should note the ways in which children are acknowledging or defending against painful feelings, which may lead to defiant aggression or withdrawal. Subsequent reviews of the child's progress can then be looking for signs of increasing trust, capacity to express feelings, pleasure in activities and increased confidence.

Trust

Does the child:

- seek comfort appropriately when stressed (e.g. signal their needs verbally or physically, rather than: shut down on feelings; cling, demand and resist comfort; appear helpless; try to control others)?

- accept comfort when stressed/relax?

- use a caregiver as a secure base for exploration (i.e. after accepting reassurance or comfort, become able to explore and play)?

- have a selective attachment to one or more caregiver?

- protest at separation from caregiver?

- settle to play at reunion after separation?

- show interest and pleasure in the environment (enjoy the senses – bright colours, taste, touch)?

- enjoy playing independently with toys?

- use their mobility and language to explore, to have fun, to approach others, to learn?

Managing feelings

Does the child:

- express a range of positive and negative feelings but not be overwhelmed by them (NB toddlers often swing between moods – but it is the degree that counts)?

- name simple feelings?

- use language to communicate needs, feelings, ideas and goals openly and accurately (NB language abilities will vary)?

- ever pretend to feel what they are not feeling – seem false (NB this can start as young as 18 months)?

- understand that others have thoughts, feelings and goals that differ from their own?

- show empathy for others?

- show some understanding of acceptable and unacceptable behaviour (moral development)?

Self-esteem

Does the child:

- enjoy play and activities?

- take pleasure in doing something well?

- enjoy praise?

- cope with not being successful at a task/not winning sometimes?

- cope with being told off without extreme reactions?

Feeling effective

Does the child:

- make simple choices?

- show persistence in completing tasks?

- co-operate and negotiate?

- manage increased independence without excessive assertiveness/ oppositional behaviour?

- enjoy/manage sleeping, eating, toileting appropriate to his age?

- manage peer group relationships (e.g. prosocial, increasingly co-operative, making and keeping friends)?

Sense of belonging

Does the child:

- recognise and show special interest in foster/adoptive family members?

- have a sense of belonging to the foster/adoptive family?

- enjoy family occasions?

- have a sense of connection/belonging to the birth family (e.g. can recognise them in photographs)?

- react positively to contact (where relevant) with birth family members?

MIDDLE CHILDHOOD: 5 – 10 YEARS

The tasks of this age period focus on managing the developing sense of self in the context of learning and following the social rules, especially within the peer group. Thus, self-esteem, self-efficacy and co-operation become important, though as ever within the context of an available secure base caregiver to whom a child can turn when the pressures of the playground or the classroom get too much. For fostered and adopted children, the expectation in school that they will be ready to learn may not be in keeping with their capacity to concentrate, to manage the challenge of new relationships, and to cope with success and failure.

The importance of a sense of *belonging* and family membership in this age range will be marked, as children are learning how to place themselves in relation to other people within the family, in school, in activities and in society more generally. Fostered and adopted children in this age period are likely to be asking questions about their situation, and in particular why their family is different from other children's families. This does not indicate a problem in the family, but is a normal and appropriate developmental stage.

Trust

Does the child:

- seek comfort/help from other people appropriately (when needed but not excessively – balancing dependency and autonomy)?

- have a selective attachment to particular caregivers?

- use a caregiver as a secure base, i.e. seek comfort, have his anxiety reduced and then explore/learn/play?

- trust people outside the family appropriately (e.g. teachers, activity leaders, peer group)?

- indiscriminately seek out/show affection to others?

- manage friendships with peers their own age successfully?

Managing feelings

Does the child:

- show a full range of basic feelings appropriately for their age (e.g. happiness, sadness, anger) without being overwhelmed by them?

- communicate their feelings accurately in ways that can get their needs met?

- talk about/reflect on their feelings; make connections to behaviour?

- talk about/reflect on the feelings of other people; make connections to behaviour?

- show empathy for other children?

- show more complex emotions of guilt, shame or remorse – and the wish to make things better?

- understand and accept the rules at home and at school?

- have effective strategies for managing their feelings and behaviour?

Self-esteem

Does the child:

- have positive self-esteem – think he is good at some things and accept not being good at others?

- respond positively to praise at home or at school?

- take a pride in their appearance?

- feel positive about their school performance?

- get involved in organised activities or hobbies?

- gain pleasure and satisfaction from activities?

- cope with the stresses of competing with others, academically and socially?

- cope with failure and disappointment?

- cope with being told off, i.e. not despairing, shutting down or becoming aggressive?

Feeling effective

Does the child:

- make choices?

- assert himself appropriately and enjoy co-operation?

- feel effective and confident – in the family and/or with peers?

- follow through and complete tasks?

- look after their things appropriately?

Sense of belonging

Does the child:

- seem comfortable spending time with the foster/adoptive family?

- seem willing/happy to be involved in family events?

- see himself as part of the foster/adoptive family?

- see himself as part of/connected to the birth family (appropriate to placement type and circumstances)?

- talk about the birth family in a realistic and balanced way?

- tell a coherent story of their childhood and family life that makes sense to him and is realistic?

ADOLESCENCE: 11 – 18 YEARS

In assessment, it is helpful to separate early from late adolescence. In many ways, the transition from 11–15 is as critical as the transitions of the early years as young people negotiate puberty and changing family and social expectations in the process of becoming young teenagers. Assessment should focus on the extent to which the child is secure and psychologically robust enough to manage this step forward towards adulthood without loss of self-esteem – a special risk at around 12–13 years old.

The external environment for fostered and adopted young adolescents becomes a source of exciting opportunities, but also challenges and risks, as they face expectations to achieve at school alongside the increasing importance of the peer group. Self-esteem and self-efficacy are significant here, but so also is the negotiation of identity and family membership.

Older adolescents, aged 16–18, still need a secure base that provides emotional support with availability of attachment figures and a sense of belonging/family membership. The transition to adulthood will need a whole range of personal, cognitive and emotional skills and resources, as well as external supports from families, friends and, where necessary, professionals.

Trust

Does the young person:

- seek comfort/help from other people appropriately while also becoming increasingly independent?

- have a selective attachment to a particular caregiver?

- use a caregiver (or other adult) as a secure base (e.g. seek comfort, have his anxiety reduced and then be confident to explore and learn)?

- trust people outside the family appropriately (e.g. teachers, activity leaders, peer groups)?

- discriminate between familiar people and strangers in seeking out/showing affection to others?

Managing feelings

Does the young person:

- express a range of feelings appropriately?

- manage difficult feelings without being overwhelmed by them or denying them?

- manage feelings and relationships appropriately with their peer group?

- have a close confiding relationship with at least one friend?

- think about/reflect on their own feelings and behaviour?

- think about/reflect on other people's feelings and behaviour?

- have constructive strategies for managing their feelings and behaviour (e.g. using others for support rather than resorting to substance misuse, self-harm, etc)?

Self-esteem

Does the young person:

- have positive self-esteem – think he is good at some things and accept that he cannot be good at everything?

- engage in purposeful activity that can offer a sense of identity and self-esteem?

- enjoy learning and/or new activities?

- take pride in his appearance and feel positive about his school performance?

- get involved in organised activities or hobbies?

- gain pleasure and satisfaction from activities?

- manage the stresses of competing with others, academically and socially?

- cope with failure and disappointment (i.e. can think it through, remain positive)?

- cope with being told off (i.e. not despairing, shutting down or becoming aggressive)?

Feeling effective

Does the young person:

- think through options and make appropriate choices?

- feel competent to get his needs met?

- assert themselves appropriately?

- co-operate with parents and other authority figures?
- co-operate with peers – friends and siblings?

Sense of belonging

Does the young person:

- have at least one supportive family to belong to?
- see themselves as part of the foster/adoptive family?
- see themselves as connected to/part of the birth family (appropriate to placement type)?
- have a balanced sense of identity in relation to their peer group, e.g. value their opinions but can be true to themselves?

Frequently Asked Questions

Q: How is Secure Base being used in practice?

A: Local authorities and independent fostering and adoption agencies are using the model to support their work at all stages from assessment of children and recruitment to matching, support and transition to adulthood. They use it in their work with foster carers, adoptive parents, looked after and adopted children and young people, and birth parents.

Q: Can I use just one dimension of the model? For instance, if a child has low self-esteem, can I focus simply on "acceptance"?

A: It may be useful to start with a particular dimension identified with the caregiver, but we think that the model is most productive if all dimensions are covered. This is because all of the dimensions are connected and it is hard to completely separate any single one. For example, building self-esteem will involve accepting the child for who he is, but it is also likely to involve the caregiver being available to the child, being sensitive to how the child is feeling, and working co-operatively with the child to promote success. Self-esteem may also be promoted through feeling "part of the family" and through a family culture of acceptance of strengths and limitations. So as suggested in the Secure Base star, each dimension interacts with and contributes to the others.

Q: Does the model apply to older children and teenagers?

A: Yes. Sometimes practitioners think of attachment as a theory that is mainly useful for working with babies and young children, but it is just as important for older children and adolescents. People of all ages need to be able to rely on a secure base to support their exploration and as a safe haven to be there for them at times of stress and anxiety. In fact, young people in transition to adulthood are particularly in need of a reliable secure base as they face new challenges. The key issue is the capacity of the caregiver to communicate messages of availability, sensitivity and so on in ways that are acceptable and age-appropriate for the young person.

Q: Does the model apply to black and minority ethnic children and young people?

A: Yes. The concept of a secure base is not culturally specific and all children will benefit from positive caregiving across all five of the dimensions proposed in the model. However, it may be that different cultures have different family patterns, such that members of the extended family, for example, may be more actively involved in the care of a child and may also become an active part of the child's secure base.

There may also be additional issues related to developing a strong and positive sense of ethnic and cultural identity for caregivers of both white and BME children within each dimension. For example: dealing with various types of prejudice, including racism, may require additional emotional and physical availability; particular sensitivity may be needed to tune in to the feelings of a child who has been dislocated from their cultural background or who has little information about their heritage. Careful attention will need to be paid to helping all children to gain knowledge of and feel pride in their culture and ethnicity as this is key to positive self-esteem and the experience of having a secure base.

Q: Can the model be used for a child who has been diagnosed with an attachment disorder?

A: Even where children have more extreme difficulties in close relationships, the principles of this model still apply. What has to be borne in mind, however, is that when caring for children who have perhaps experienced traumatic abuse and/or recurrent separations and losses, the tasks of remaining available, being mind-minded, being accepting and co-operative may be constantly challenged by the child. So a high level of support is needed by a supervisor who understands the dimensions but also understands this additional level of need. In addition, even where a child may be having regular therapy sessions, their day-to-day life and experience of caregiving in a family still needs to help them to build trust in caregivers and to learn to regulate their feelings and behaviour.

The Secure Base can assist caregivers in defining what aspects of their caregiving may be most helpful and in seeing even small signs of progress on the dimensions. In fact, the concept of "providing a secure base" within the family and professional network may be more useful for those children who find it most difficult to engage in close relationships, than aiming to "build a secure attachment" in the first instance. This is because the Secure Base model widens the focus from the one-to-one relationship with a parental caregiver to thinking about how other areas of the child's life, such as the extended foster or adoptive family, school and activities, could contribute to an increased sense of security and resilience.

Q: Do I have permission to use the Secure Base practice resources?

A: Because caregivers and social work professionals have found these ideas and resources helpful, we want to make them readily available. There are two simple conditions for their use:

1. The source of the materials should be acknowledged, i.e. Secure Base, Gillian Schofield and Mary Beek, Centre for Research on Children and Families, University of East Anglia, Norwich, UK – with BAAF publications referenced appropriately.

2. The core concepts and elements of the Secure Base (that is, the model itself and the cycles) should not be changed. But using fresh examples in training that come from experience and illustrate each dimension or generate a wider range of approaches to caregiving are an important part of making Secure Base remain relevant to practice.

Q: What training or preparation is necessary for me or for foster carers and adopters to be able to use the Secure Base?

A: Training is not essential and you will be able to use Secure Base with foster carers or adopters simply by reading this book carefully. You may wish also to draw on key chapters in the *Attachment Handbook for Foster Care and Adoption* (Schofield and Beek, 2006) for more detailed knowledge of attachment and resilience theory as they relate to child development and caregiving. Opportunities for training on Secure Base may also be available from BAAF's trainers and other sources within agencies.

Q: Reading this material has raised personal questions and reactions about my own childhood or my own caregiving approach. How should I deal with these?

A: It is common for attachment-related material to raise personal questions and concerns. As when cases you are working with raise personal issues, it is important to consider discussing them with your line manager or with trusted colleagues – or contacting a professional in your local area. For social workers, and for foster carers or adopters, exploring and dealing with personal issues that may arise should be seen as a positive opportunity for professional and personal growth.

References

Ainsworth MDS, Bell S and Stayton D (1971) 'Individual differences in strange-situation behaviour of one-year-olds', in Schaffer H (ed) *The Origins of Human Social Relations,* New York, NY: Academic Press, pp. 17–52

Ainsworth MDS, Blehar M, Waters E and Wall S (1978) *Patterns of Attachment: A psychological study of the Strange Situation,* Hillsdale, NJ: Lawrence Erlbaum

Beek M and Schofield G (2004) *Providing a Secure Base in Long-Term Foster Care*, London: BAAF

Bowlby J (1969/82) *Attachment and Loss: Vol I Attachment,* London: Hogarth Press

Bowlby J (1973) *Attachment and Loss: Vol II Separation, Anxiety and Anger,* London: Hogarth Press

Bowlby J (1980) *Attachment and Loss: Vol III Loss, Sadness and Depression,* London: Hogarth Press

Bowlby J (1988) *A Secure Base: Clinical applications of attachment theory,* London: Routledge

Cairns B (2004) *Fostering Attachments*, London: BAAF

Crittenden PM (1995) 'Attachment and psychopathology', in Goldberg S, Muir R and Kerr J (eds) *Attachment Theory: Social developmental and clinical perspectives*, Hillsdale, NJ: Analytical Press, pp. 367–406

Howe D (2005) *Child Abuse and Neglect: Attachment, development and intervention*, Basingstoke: Macmillan

Howe D (2011) *Attachment Across the Life Course: A brief introduction*, Basingstoke: Macmillan

Main M and Hesse E (1990) 'Parents' unresolved traumatic experiences are related to infant disorganised attachment status: is frightened and/or frightening the linking mechanism?', in Greenberg MT and Cummings EM (eds) *Attachment in the Preschool Years: Theory, research and intervention*, Chicago, IL: University of Chicago Press, pp. 161–182

Main M and Solomon J (1986) 'Discovery of an insecure/disorganised/disoriented attachment pattern', in Braselton TB and Yogwan MW (eds) *Affective Development in Infancy*, Norwood, NJ: Ablex, pp. 95–124

Meins E, Fermyhough C, Wainwright R, Clark-Carter D, Das Gupta M, Fradley E and Tuckey M (2003) 'Pathways to understanding mind: construct of maternal validity and predictive validity of natural mind-mindedness' in *Child Development,* 14:4, pp. 637–648

Schofield G, Beek H, Sargent K and Thoburn J (2000) *Growing up in Foster Care*, London: BAAF

Schofield G and Beek M (2006) *Attachment Handbook for Foster Care and Adoption*, London: BAAF

Schofield G and Beek M (2009) 'Growing up in foster care: providing a secure base through adolescence', *Child and Family Social Work*, 14:3, pp. 255–266

Sunderland M (2000) *Helping Children with Feelings* (resource pack), Bicester: Speechmark Publishing

Wilson K, Sinclair I and Petrie S (2003) 'A kind of loving: a model of effective foster care', *British Journal of Social Work*, 33, pp. 991–1003

Secure Base Summary Chart

AVAILABILITY – helping the child to trust	SENSITIVITY – helping the child to manage feelings	ACCEPTANCE – building the child's self-esteem	CO-OPERATION – helping the child to feel effective	FAMILY MEMBERSHIP – helping the child to belong

CAREGIVER THINKING

What does this child expect from adults? How can I show this child that I will not let him/her down?	What might this child be thinking and feeling? How does this child make me feel?	I need to value and accept myself.	This child needs to feel effective and competent. How can we work together?	This child is part of my family and also connected to their birth family.

CAREGIVING BEHAVIOUR

Alert to child's needs/signals. Verbal and non-verbal messages of availability.	Helping the child to understand and manage feelings appropriately.	Helping the child to feel good about him/herself and manage setbacks.	Promoting competence, offering choice. Negotiating within firm boundaries.	Verbal and non-verbal messages of connection to both families.

CHILD'S THINKING AND FEELING

I matter. I am safe. I can explore and return for help. Other people can be trusted.	My feelings make sense and can be managed. Other people have thoughts and feelings.	I am accepted and valued for who I am. I do not have to be perfect.	I feel effective. I can make choices. I can co-operate with others.	I have a sense of belonging. I can feel connected to more than one family.

CHILD'S BEHAVIOUR

Uses carer as a secure base for exploration.	Reflects on feelings of self and others. Regulates feelings and is empathic.	Shows realistic but positive appraisal of self.	Is appropriately assertive. Negotiates and co-operates.	Manages the connection to one or more families.

Secure Base Progress Record

Name of child:

Date of birth:

1. Availability – helping the child to trust

Date	Behaviour that shows the child's ability or inability to trust/to use caregiver(s) as a secure base	Suggested approaches to build on strengths and help with difficulties in this dimension	Change/progress

2. Sensitivity – helping the child to manage feelings

Date	Behaviour that shows the child's ability or inability to manage their feelings	Suggested approaches to build on strengths and help with difficulties in this dimension	Change/progress

3. Acceptance – building the child's self-esteem

Date	Behaviour that shows the child's self-esteem, ability or inability to enjoy success and manage setbacks	Suggested approaches to build on strengths and help with difficulties in this dimension	Change/progress

4. Co-operation – helping the children to feel effective

Date	Behaviour that shows the child's ability or inability to make choices, feel effective, be co-operative	Suggested approaches to build on strengths and help with difficulties in this dimension	Change/progress

5. Family membership – helping the child to belong

Date	Behaviour that shows whether the child feels a comfortable sense of belonging in your family/connection to their birth family	Suggested approaches to build on strengths and help with difficulties in this dimension	Change/progress

Secure Base star

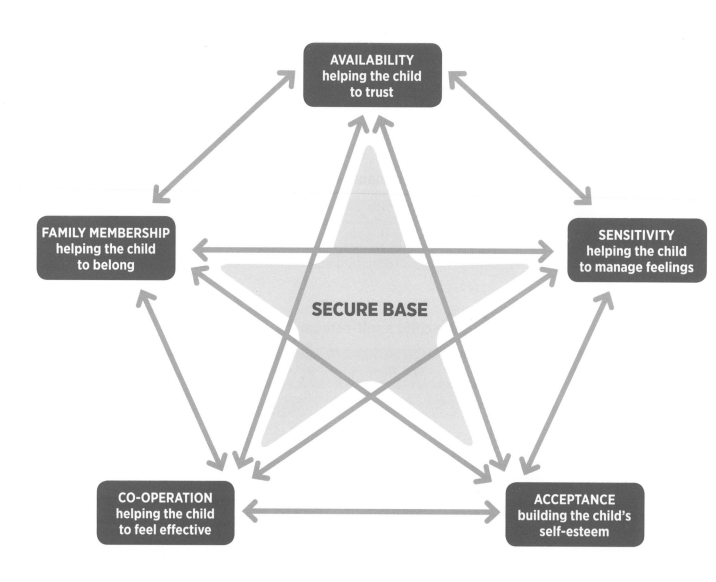

Secure Base – caregiving cycle and dimensions

The caregiving cycle

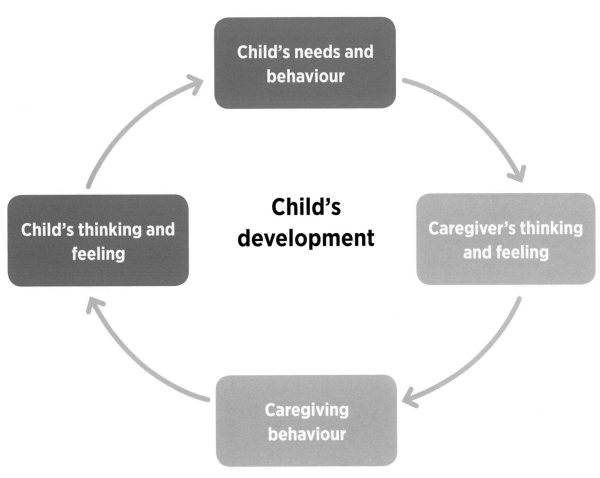

Availability

Sensitivity

Child's needs and behaviour

Child thinking/ feeling

My feelings make sense and can be managed

Other people have thoughts and feelings

Helping the child to manage feelings

Caregiver thinking/ feeling

What might this child be thinking and feeling?

How does this child make me feel?

Helping the child to understand, express and manage feelings appropriately

Caregiving behaviour

Acceptance

Co-operation

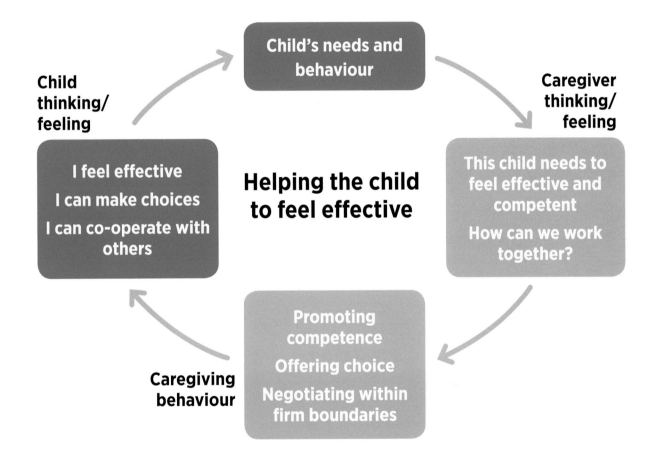

Child thinking/ feeling

Child's needs and behaviour

Caregiver thinking/ feeling

I feel effective

I can make choices

I can co-operate with others

Helping the child to feel effective

This child needs to feel effective and competent

How can we work together?

Caregiving behaviour

Promoting competence

Offering choice

Negotiating within firm boundaries

Family membership

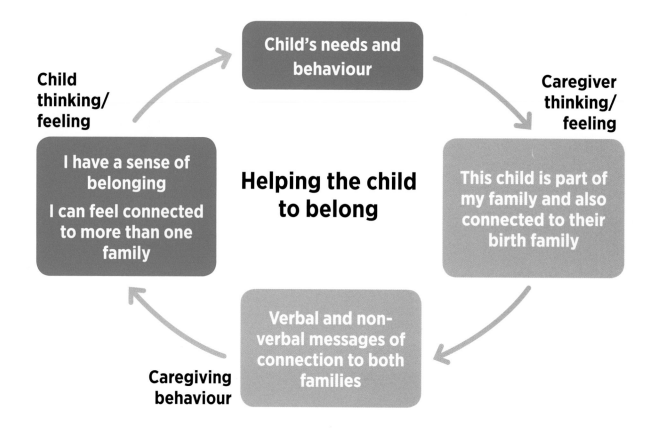

Child's needs and behaviour

Child thinking/ feeling

I have a sense of belonging

I can feel connected to more than one family

Helping the child to belong

Caregiver thinking/ feeling

This child is part of my family and also connected to their birth family

Caregiving behaviour

Verbal and non-verbal messages of connection to both families

Secure Base – Guide to the DVD

The DVD that accompanies this guide provides us with examples to illustrate each of the five Secure Base dimensions, as described by foster carers, adopters and young people. It demonstrates how varied caregiving may be in each dimension, for example, being available for a baby compared to being available for a teenager, or offering family membership and experiencing a sense of belonging for young people.

There are a number of ways in which the DVD can be used.

- Individual social workers, foster carers and adopters can learn from viewing the DVD how the ideas set out in this guide can be translated into sensitive caregiving – and how much young people value their experiences in supportive foster and adoptive families.

- The DVD can be used by practitioners and trainers to introduce the Secure Base model and to provide opportunities for discussion with preparation or support groups of adoptive parents or foster carers.

- The DVD can also be used by social workers working with individual carers or adopters who wish to work with Secure Base to help a particular child or young person.

The DVD can be viewed straight through but is also divided into chapters, so it is possible to view each dimension separately. The list of contents below indicates the range of contributors and briefly explains the link to the dimension.

DVD contents

Chapter 1   AVAILABILITY – HELPING THE CHILD TO TRUST

- **Vanessa:** Helping a baby to signal her needs.

- **Karen:** Helping a four-year-old child gradually to accept physical comfort and closeness.

- **Linda and Sam:** Working together to signal their availability to an angry, distressed child.

- **Morris:** Offering a hug when a wary child eventually signals his readiness.

- **Pauline:** Using different approaches to enable children to trust her and express their feelings.

- **Vanessa:** Ensuring that young children can cope with separation.

- **Karen:** Offering extra reassurance that caregivers are available during contact.

- **Gordon:** Getting a computer for a teenager – demonstrating that they will not let her down.

- **Jon and Sara:** Reflections on their experiences of availability in foster care and adoption.

Chapter 2   SENSITIVITY – HELPING THE CHILD TO MANAGE FEELINGS

- **Vanessa:** Describing how a child can bottle up feelings that a carer needs to understand.

- **Dolores:** Standing in the child's shoes, drawing on her own experience.

- **Morris:** Thinking about his own childhood experiences of sibling arguments – helping children to manage their own feelings.

- **Pauline:** Helping children to share their feelings.

- **Sandy:** Finding a way of communicating concern and helping a teenager who found it hard to talk about things that were upsetting her.

- **Sam and Linda:** Helping a child to manage his feelings of anger and despair.

- **Jon:** Remembering foster carers who were attuned and responsive to his feelings.

- **Sara:** Being helped to make sense of her adoption story.

Chapter 3   ACCEPTANCE – BUILDING THE CHILD'S SELF-ESTEEM

- **Dolores:** Being proud to be who you are.

- **Sandy:** Feeling like the "Wicked Witch of the West".

- **Dolores:** Building a black child's self-esteem.

- **Chris and Roger:** Talking of the drawing talent of their long-term foster child, who is autistic.

- **Jon:** Placing great value on being supported with activities.

- **David:** Having his self-esteem raised by the encouragement of his foster mother.

- **Patrick:** Being proud of achievements and valuing the support from his foster family.

- **Sara:** Accepting her adoptive parent's message that she is loved and valued for herself.

Chapter 4   CO-OPERATION – HELPING CHILDREN TO FEEL EFFECTIVE

- **Sam and Linda:** Promoting a child's co-operation at bedtime.
- **Vanessa:** Offering choices and helping children to make decisions.
- **Sandy:** Offering choices to resolve a conflict.
- **Pauline:** Using weekly family meetings to build self-esteem.
- **David:** Being helped to think about strategies to deal effectively with a difficult situation.
- **Jon:** Remembering the co-operative alliance between himself and his foster carers.

Chapter 5   FAMILY MEMBERSHIP – HELPING CHILDREN TO BELONG

- **Dolores:** Offering a sense of welcome and inclusion.
- **Nancy:** Ensuring that foster children feel fully included.
- **Nancy:** Making a permanent commitment to a child.
- **Nancy:** Using the Christmas period to keep in touch with previous foster children.
- **Dolores and Morris:** Offering a family base to their now adult foster children.
- **Patrick, Sarah and Jon:** Finding a sense of belonging in their foster or adoptive families.
- **Pauline:** Helping adopted children to manage their birth family identities.
- **Chris and Roger:** Doing life story work with children with disabilities.
- **Nancy:** Valuing a foster son's close relationship with his birth parents.
- **Pauline:** Being positive about birth parents.
- **Sarah:** Describing the importance of life story work.
- **Jon:** Being supported to manage his membership of more than one family at his own pace.